CITY OF KAWARTHA LAKES

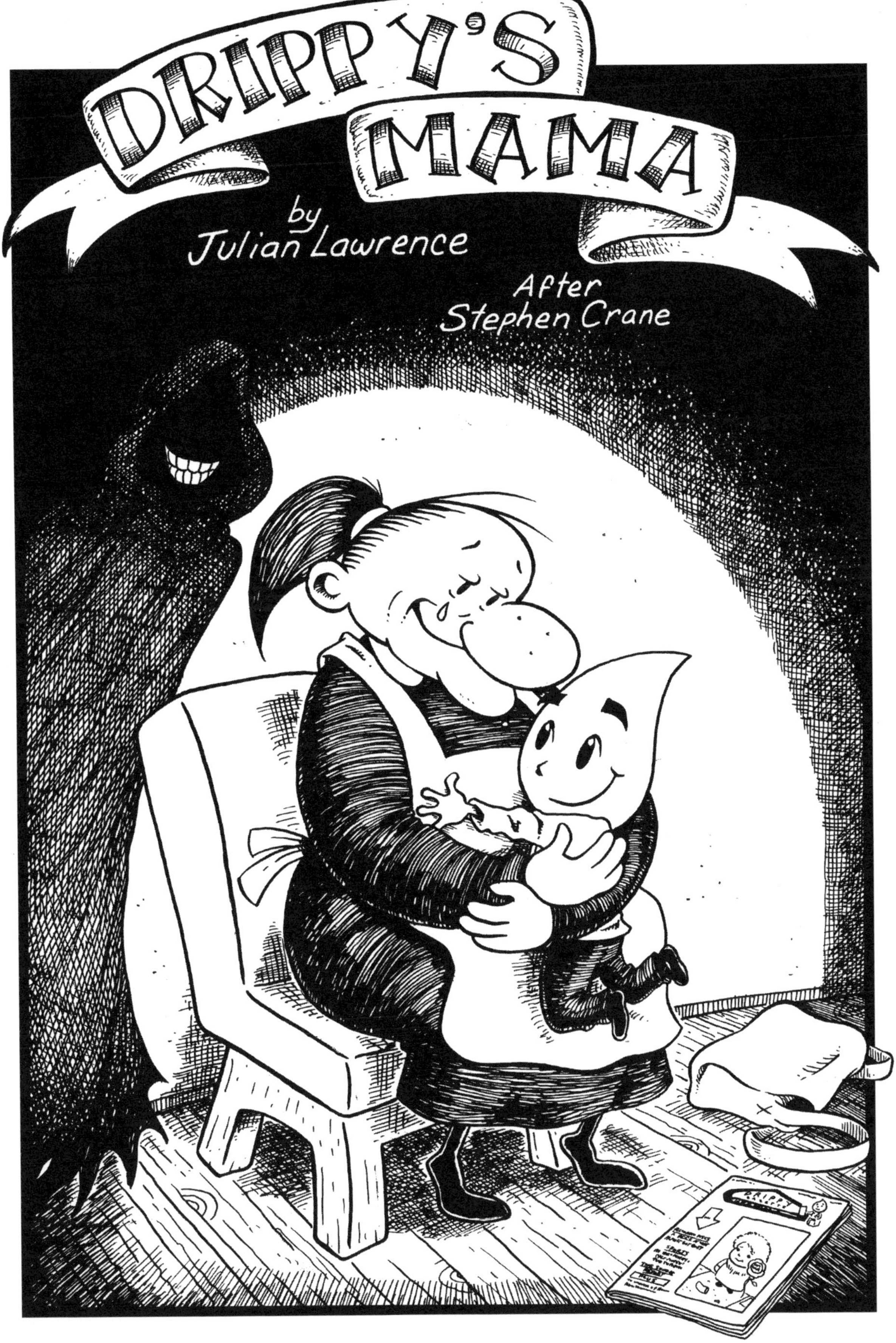
DRIPPY'S
MAMA
by
Julian Lawrence
After
Stephen Crane

Library and Archives Canada Cataloguing in Publication

Lawrence, Julian, author
    Drippy's mama /Julian Lawrence

(The adventures of Drippy the newsboy; 1)
Contents: Volume 1. Drippy's mama
ISBN 978-1-894994-94-1 (v.1: pbk.)

    1. Graphic novels. I. Title.

PN6733.L39D75 2015   741.5'971   C2015-900854-9

Conundrum Press
Greenwich, Nova Scotia, Canada
www.conundrumpress.com

Conundrum Press acknowledges the financial support of
the Canada Council for the Arts and the Government of Canada
through the Canada Book Fund, toward its publishing activities.

Canada Council
for the Arts

Conseil des Arts
du Canada

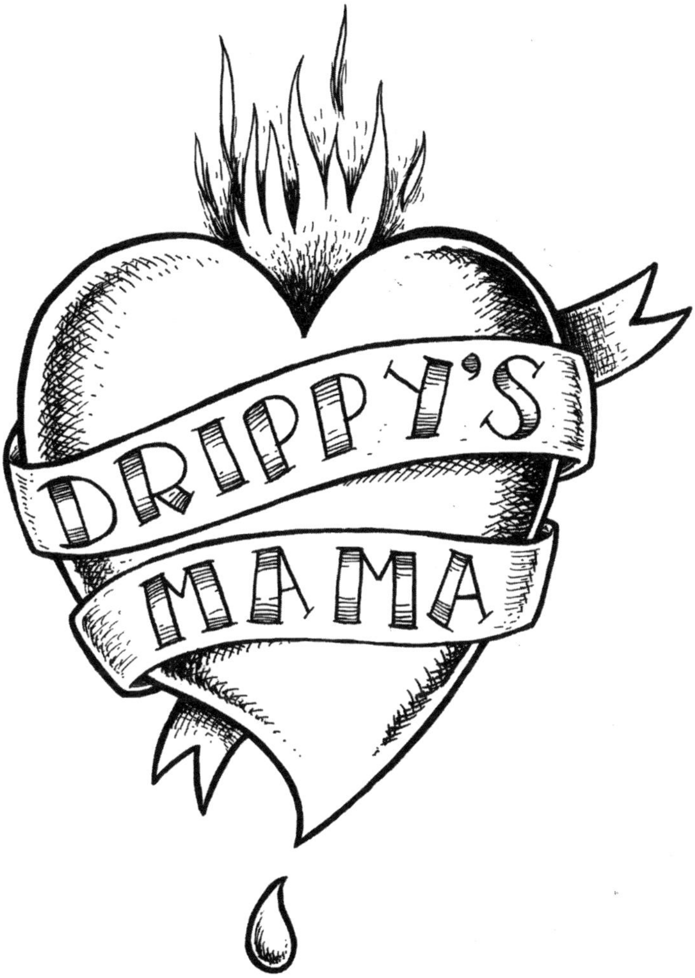
DRIPPY'S
MAMA

By Julian Lawrence

Based on the novel *George's Mother* by Stephen Crane

For all mothers...

and Robert Dayton Alexis Gall, Lester Smolenski & Ted Dave
Thank you
JULIAN

I sell th'mornin' paper my name's Drippy I walk around--
Ever'body knows that I'm th' newsboy of Drippytown.
You'll hear me yell: "Drippy Gazette!" as I run along th'street
I have no hat upon my head, no shoes upon my feet.
I'm awful cold and hungry sir, my clothes are torn'n'thin
I wander'bout from place to place my daily bread to win.
Never mind, ma'm, how I look, don't look at me and frown
I sell th' mornin' papers sir, all over Drippytown.
My father died a drunkard sir, I've heard my Mama say
An' I'm helpin' Mama, sir, as I journey on my way.
Mama always tells me ma'm,
There's nothin' in this world to lose
I'll get a place in Heaven sir, to sell th' Gospel News.
I sell th'mornin' paper my name's Drippy I walk around--
Ever'body knows that I'm th' newsboy of Drippytown.

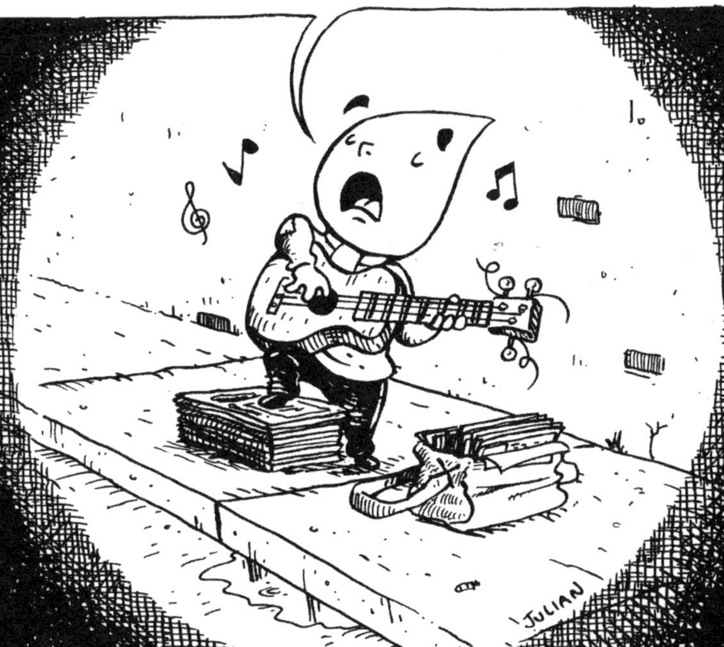
JULIAN

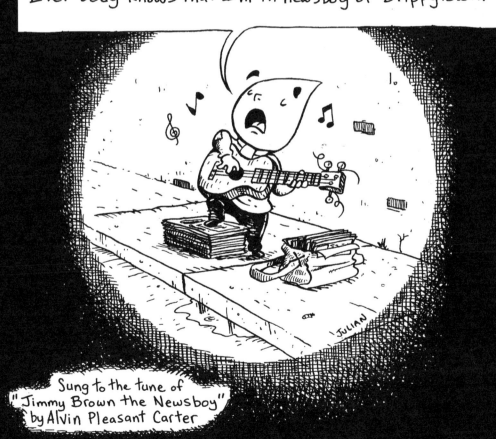

Sung to the tune of "Jimmy Brown the Newsboy" by Alvin Pleasant Carter

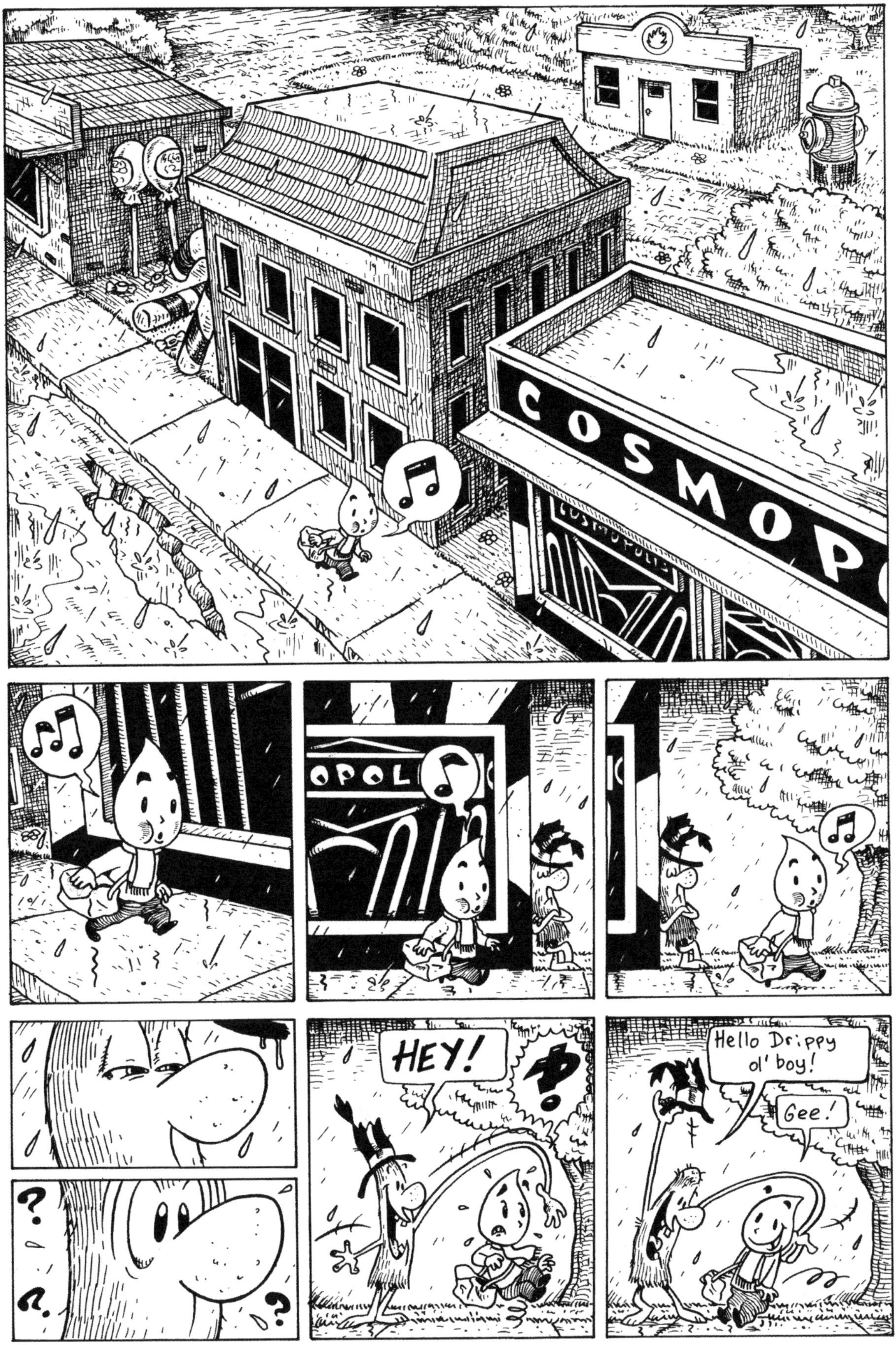
COSMOPO
COSMOPOLIS
OPOL
HEY!
Hello Drippy ol' boy!
Gee!

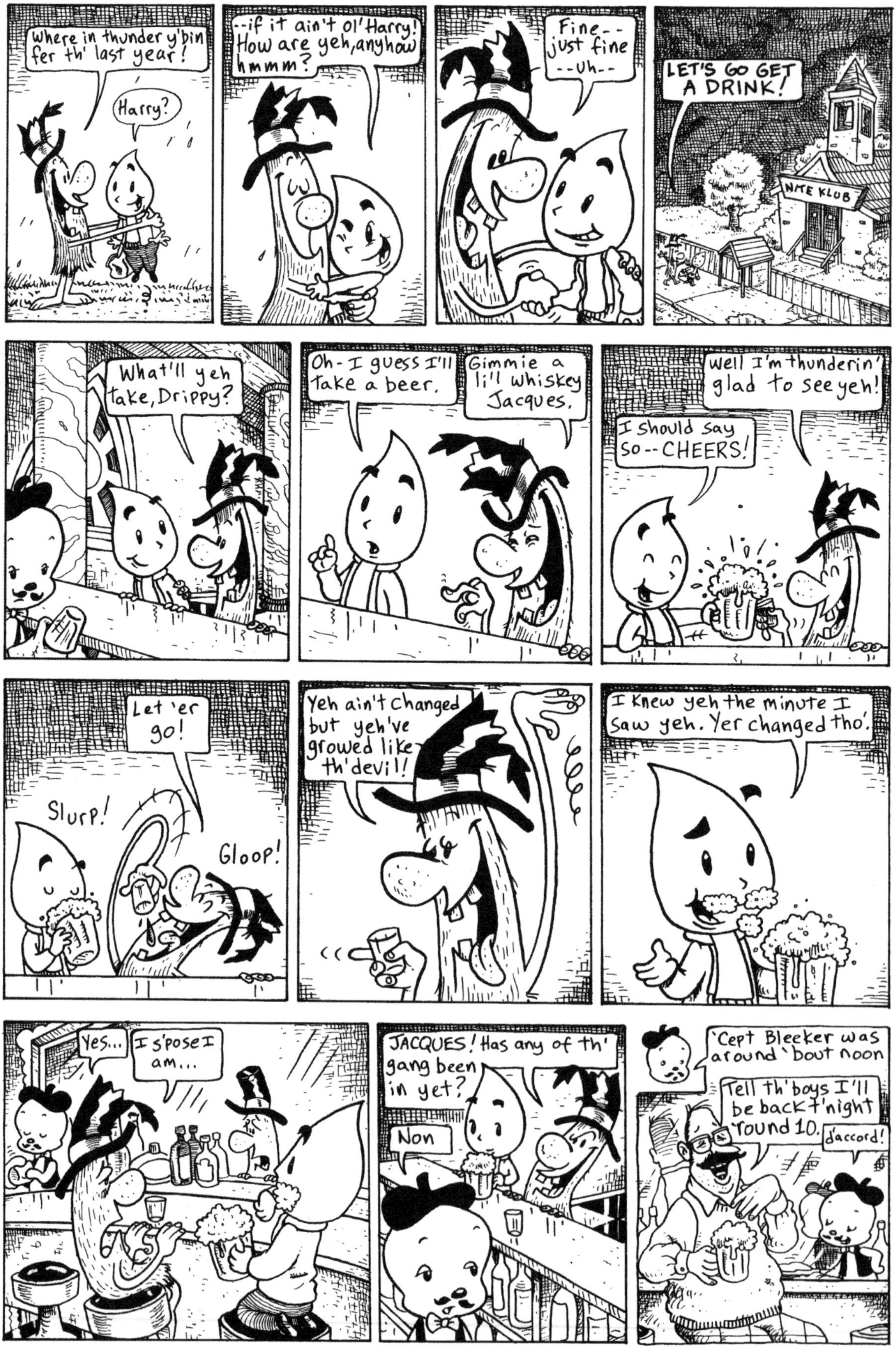
Where in thunder y'bin fer th' last year!
Harry?
--if it ain't ol' Harry! How are yeh, anyhow hmmm?
Fine-- just fine --uh--
LET'S GO GET A DRINK!
NITE KLUB
What'll yeh take, Drippy?
Oh- I guess I'll take a beer.
Gimmie a li'l whiskey Jacques.
Well I'm thunderin' glad to see yeh!
I should say so--CHEERS!
Let 'er go!
Slurp!
Gloop!
Yeh ain't changed but yeh've growed like th' devil!
I knew yeh the minute I saw yeh. Yer changed tho'.
Yes...
I s'pose I am...
JACQUES! Has any of th' gang been in yet?
Non
'Cept Bleeker was around 'bout noon
Tell th' boys I'll be back t'night 'round 10.
d'accord!

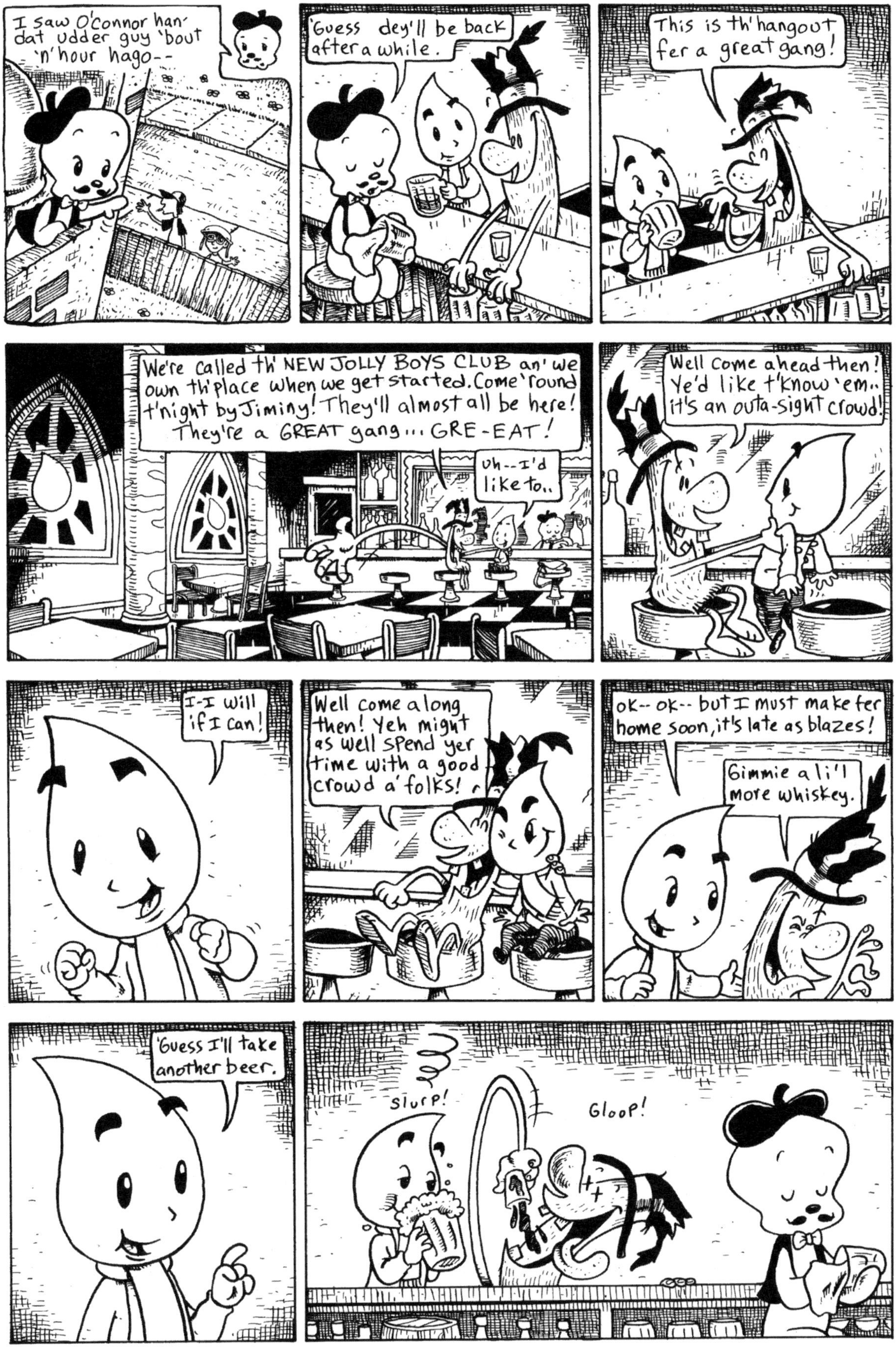
I saw O'connor han' dat udder guy 'bout 'n' hour hago--
'Guess dey'll be back after a while.
This is th' hangout fer a great gang!
We're called th' NEW JOLLY BOYS CLUB an' we own th' place when we get started. Come 'round t'night by Jiminy! They'll almost all be here! They're a GREAT gang... GRE-EAT!
Uh--I'd like to..
Well come ahead then! Ye'd like t'know 'em.. it's an outa-sight crowd!
I-I will if I can!
Well come along then! Yeh might as well spend yer time with a good crowd a' folks!
ok-- ok-- but I must make fer home soon, it's late as blazes!
Gimmie a li'l more whiskey.
'Guess I'll take another beer.
slurp!
Gloop!

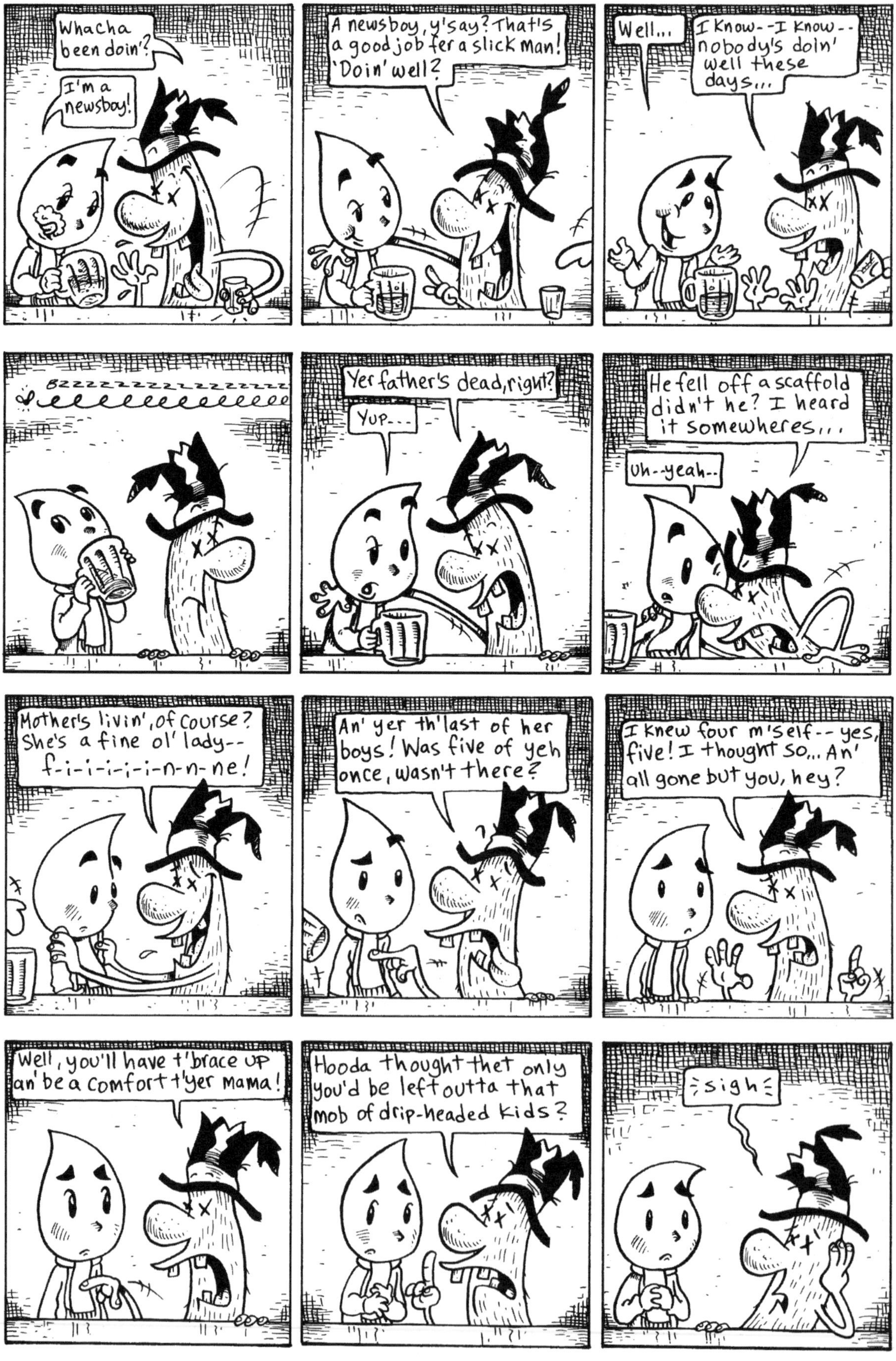
Whacha been doin'?
I'm a newsboy!
A newsboy, y'say? That's a good job fer a slick man! 'Doin' well?
Well...
I know--I know--nobody's doin' well these days...
Bzzzzzzzzzzzzzzzzzz
Yer father's dead, right?
Yup...
He fell off a scaffold didn't he? I heard it somewheres...
Uh--yeah..
Mother's livin', of course? She's a fine ol' lady--f-i-i-i-i-i-n-n-ne!
An' yer th'last of her boys! Was five of yeh once, wasn't there?
I knew four m'self--yes, five! I thought so... An' all gone but you, hey?
Well, you'll have t'brace up an' be a comfort t'yer mama!
Hooda thought thet only you'd be left outta that mob of drip-headed kids?
sigh

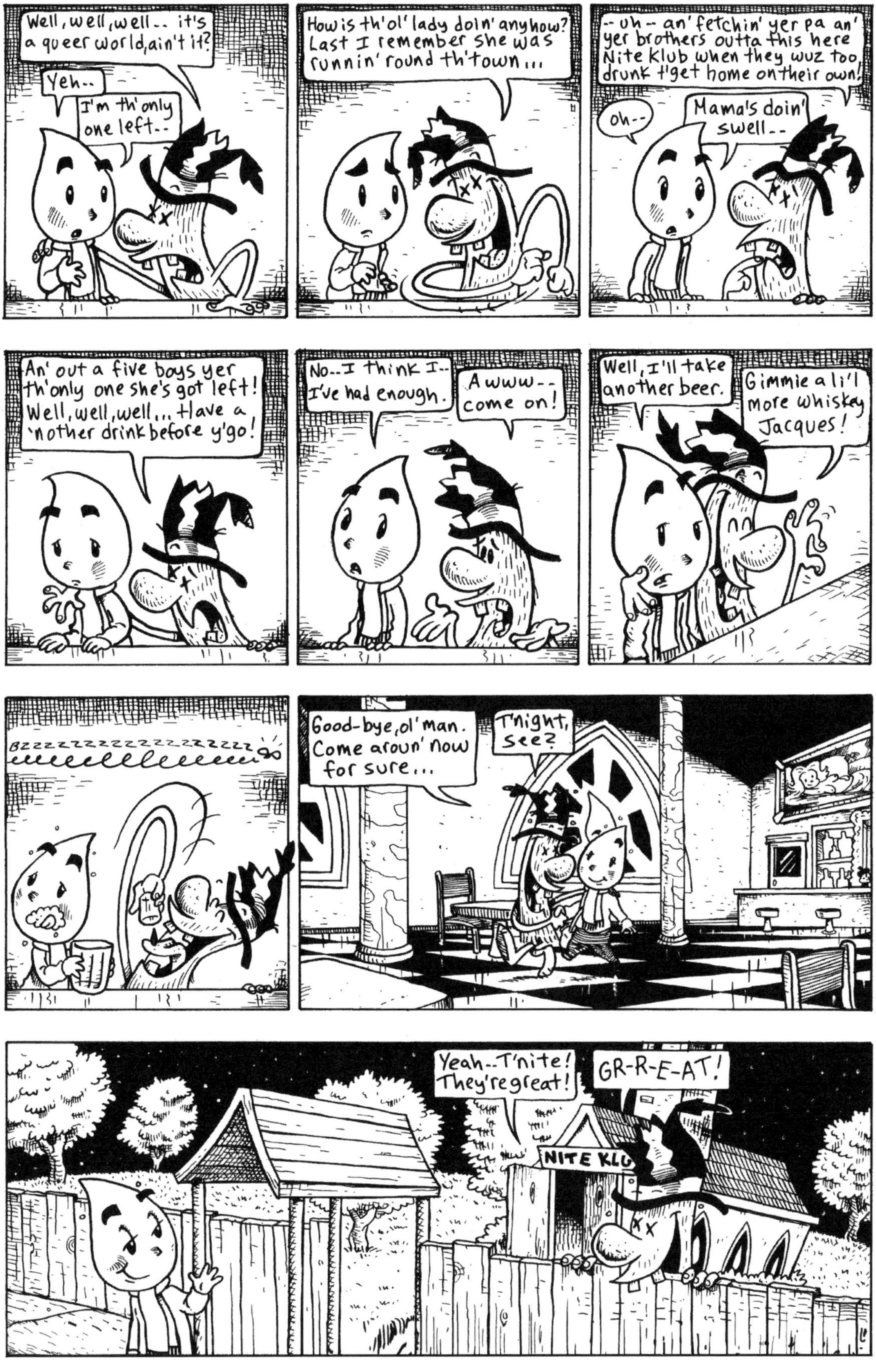

Well, well, well.. it's a queer world, ain't it?
Yeh..
I'm th' only one left..
How is th' ol' lady doin' anyhow? Last I remember she was runnin' round th' town...
-- uh -- an' fetchin' yer pa an' yer brothers outta this here Nite Klub when they wuz too drunk t'get home on their own!
Oh--
Mama's doin' swell..
An' out a five boys yer th' only one she's got left! Well, well, well... Have a 'nother drink before y'go!
No.. I think I.. I've had enough.
A www.. come on!
Well, I'll take another beer.
Gimmie a li'l more whiskey Jacques!
BZZZZZZZZZZZZZZZZZZ
Good-bye, ol' man. Come aroun' now for sure...
T'night, see?
Yeah.. T'nite! They're great!
GR-R-E-AT!
NITE KLU

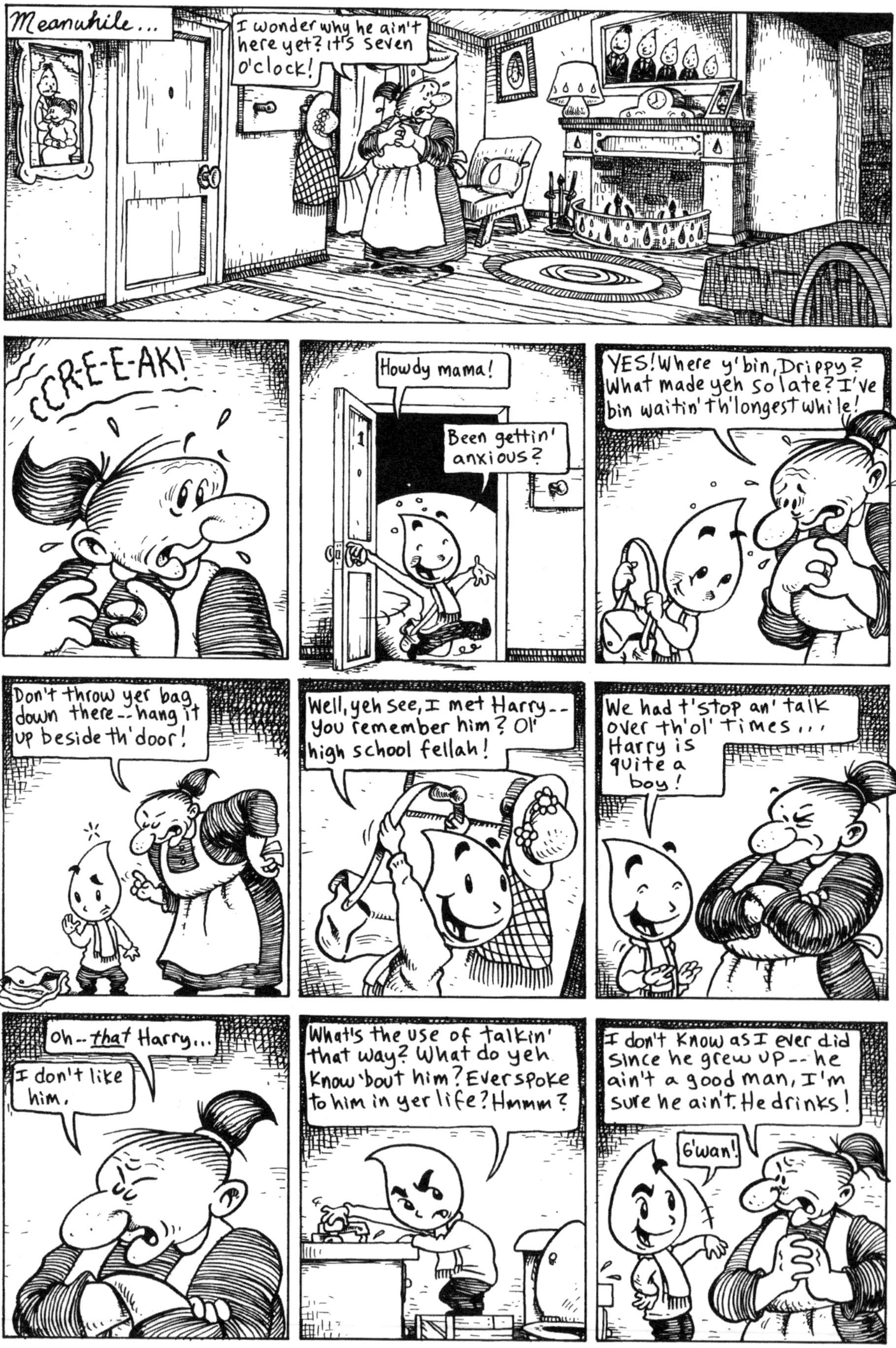
Meanwhile...
I wonder why he ain't here yet? it's seven o'clock!
CCR-E-E-AK!
Howdy mama!
Been gettin' anxious?
YES! Where y'bin, Drippy? What made yeh so late? I've bin waitin' th'longest while!
Don't throw yer bag down there--hang it up beside th'door!
Well, yeh see, I met Harry--You remember him? Ol' high school fellah!
We had t'stop an' talk over th'ol' times... Harry is quite a boy!
Oh--that Harry...
I don't like him.
What's the use of talkin' that way? What do yeh know 'bout him? Ever spoke to him in yer life? Hmmm?
I don't know as I ever did since he grew up--he ain't a good man, I'm sure he ain't. He drinks!
G'wan!

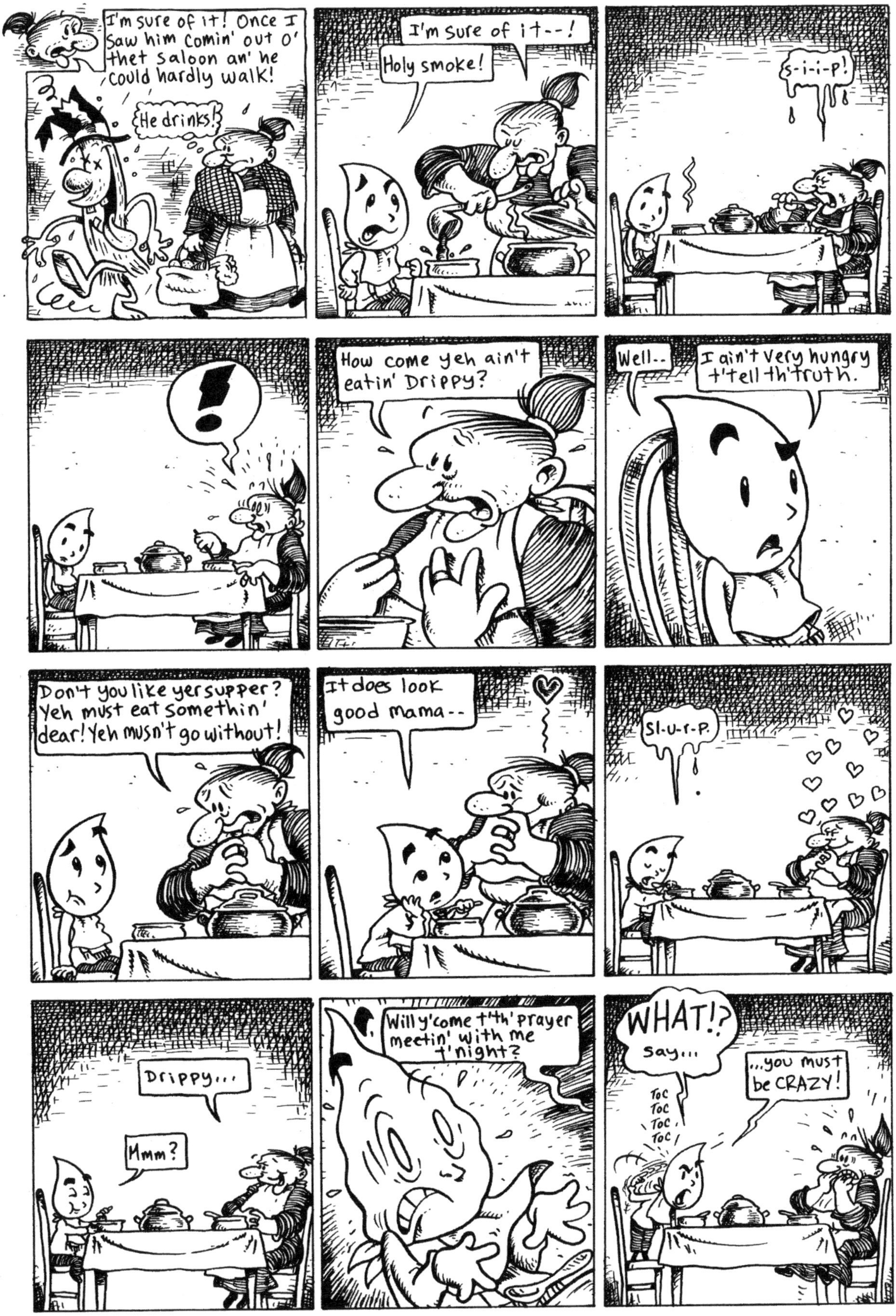
I'm sure of it! Once I saw him comin' out o' thet saloon an' he could hardly walk!
He drinks!
I'm sure of it--!
Holy smoke!
s-i-i-p!
!
How come yeh ain't eatin' Drippy?
Well..
I ain't very hungry t'tell th'truth.
Don't you like yersupper? Yeh must eat somethin' dear! Yeh musn't go without!
It does look good mama--
Sl-u-r-p.
Drippy...
Mmm?
Will y'come t'th' prayer meetin' with me t'night?
WHAT!?
say...
...you must be CRAZY!
Toc
Toc
Toc
Toc

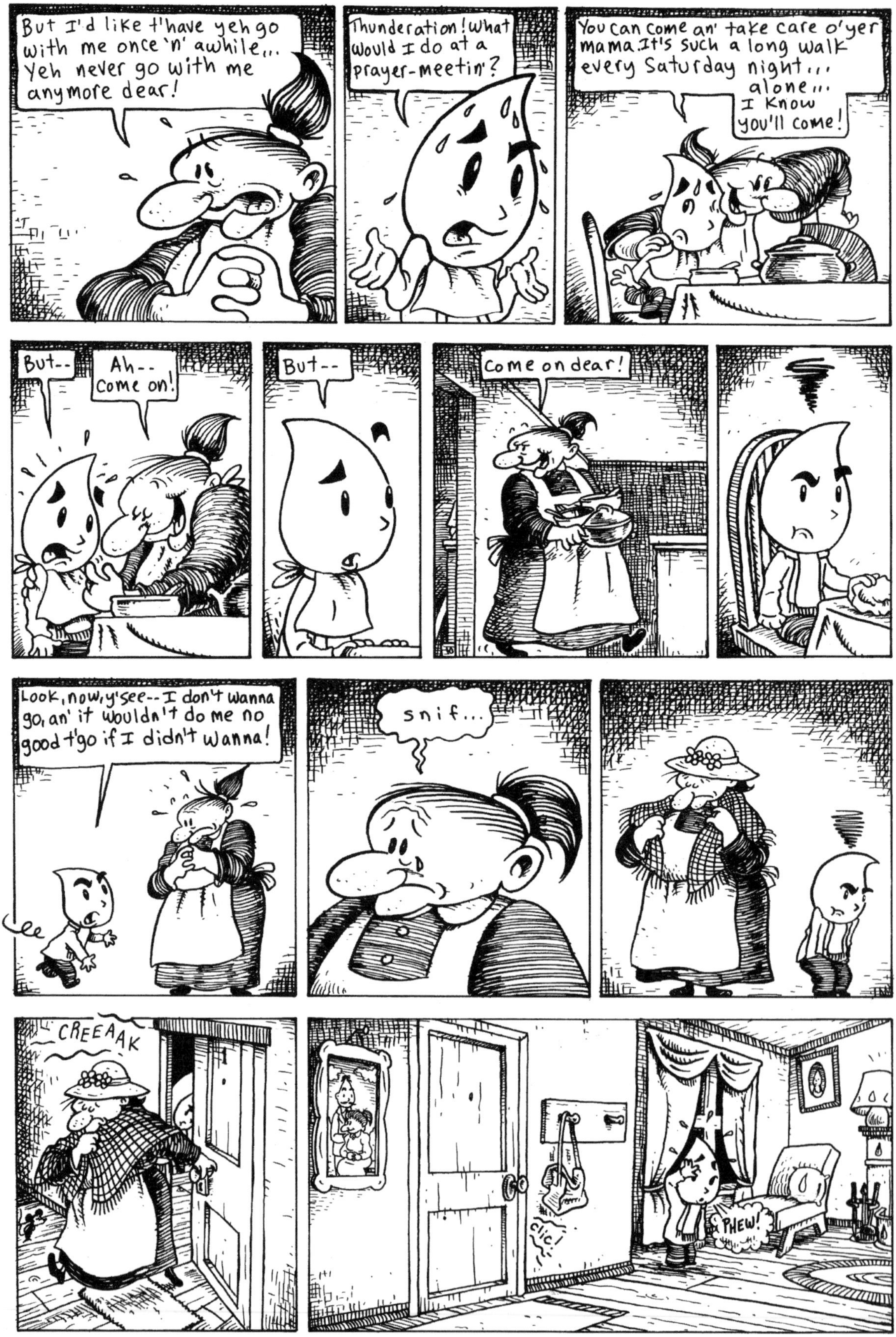
But I'd like t'have yeh go with me once 'n' awhile... Yeh never go with me anymore dear!
Thunderation! What would I do at a prayer-meetin'?
You can come an' take care o'yer mama. It's such a long walk every Saturday night... alone... I know you'll come!
But--
Ah-- come on!
But--
Come on dear!
Look, now, y'see-- I don't wanna go, an' it wouldn't do me no good t'go if I didn't wanna!
snif...
CREEAAK
clic!
PHEW!

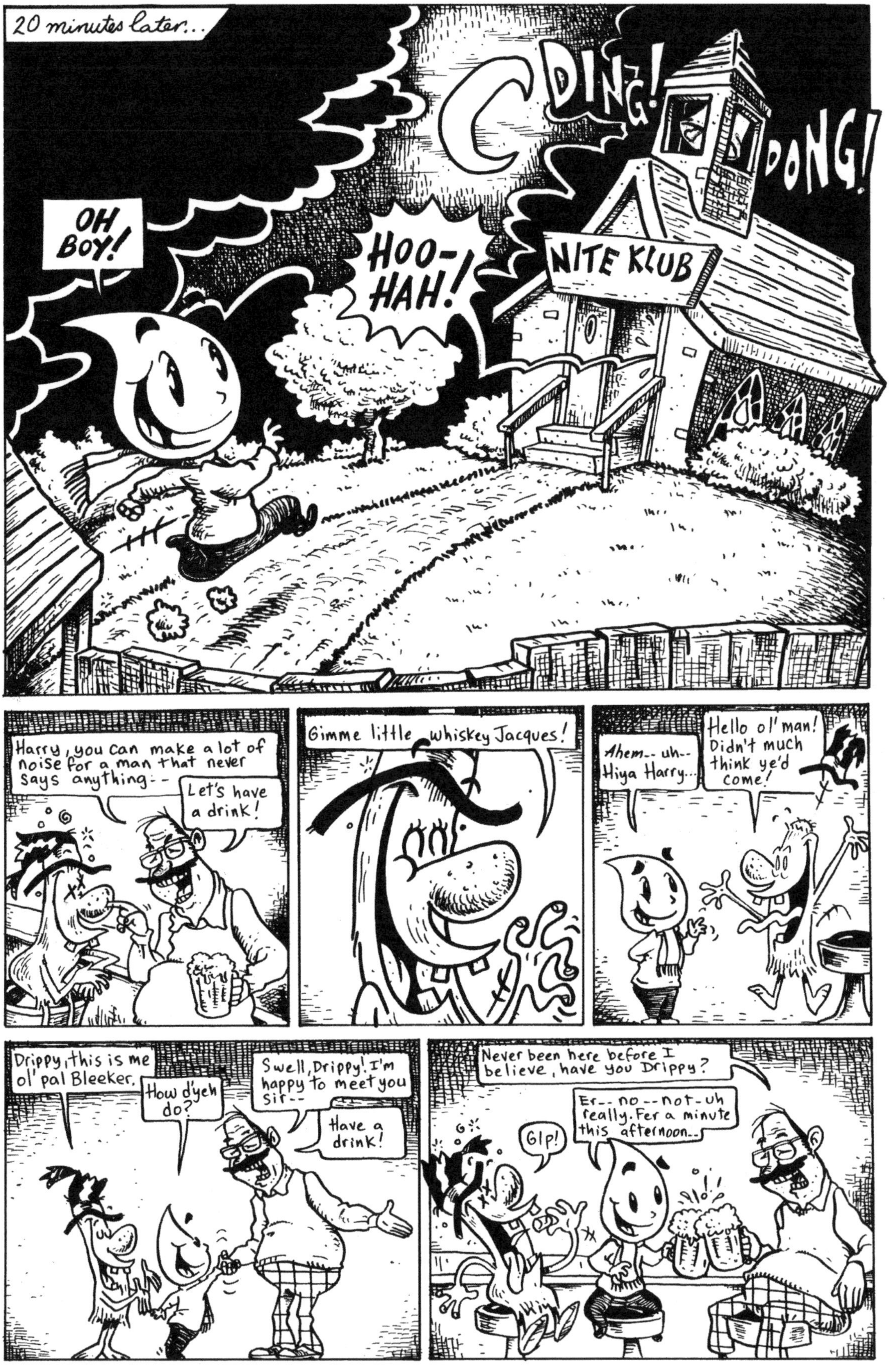
20 minutes later...
DING!
DONG!
OH BOY!
HOO-HAH!
NITE KLUB
Harry, you can make a lot of noise for a man that never says anything--
Let's have a drink!
Gimme little whiskey Jacques!
Ahem-- uh-- Hiya Harry...
Hello ol' man! Didn't much think ye'd come!
Drippy, this is me ol' pal Bleeker.
How d'yeh do?
Swell, Drippy! I'm happy to meet you sir--
Have a drink!
Never been here before I believe, have you Drippy?
Glp!
Er-- no--not-uh really. Fer a minute this afternoon..

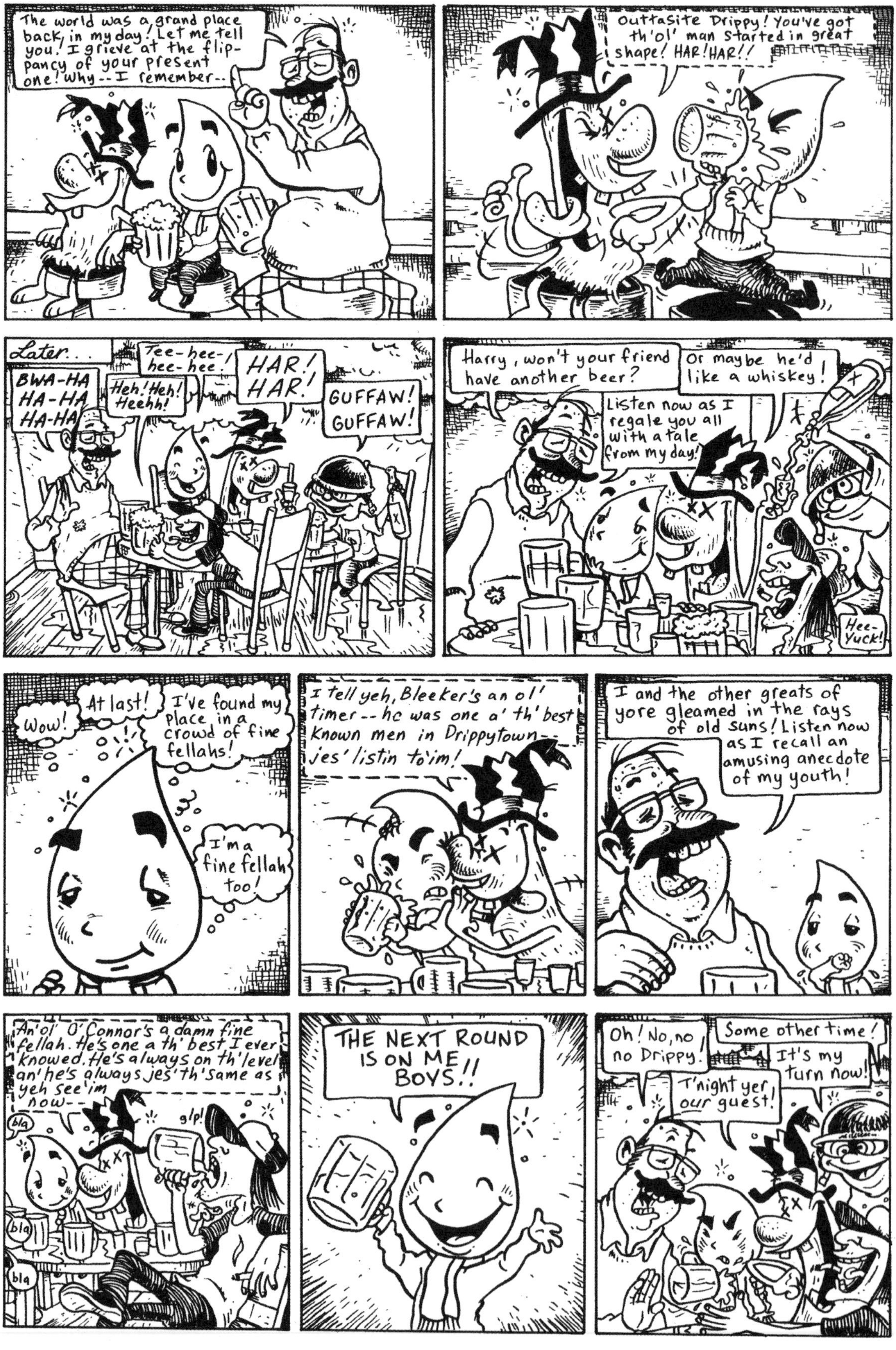

The world was a grand place back in my day! Let me tell you! I grieve at the flippancy of your present one! Why-- I remember--
Outtasite Drippy! You've got th' ol' man started in great shape! HAR! HAR!!
Later...
BWA-HA HA-HA HA-HA
Tee-hee-hee-hee!
Heh! Heh! Heehh!
HAR! HAR!
GUFFAW! GUFFAW!
Harry, won't your friend have another beer?
Or maybe he'd like a whiskey!
Listen now as I regale you all with a tale from my day!
Hee-Yuck!
Wow!
At last!
I've found my place in a crowd of fine fellahs!
I'm a fine fellah too!
I tell yeh, Bleeker's an ol' timer--he was one a' th' best known men in Drippytown-- jes' listin to'im!
I and the other greats of yore gleamed in the rays of old suns! Listen now as I recall an amusing anecdote of my youth!
An' ol' O'Connor's a damn fine fellah. He's one a th' best I ever knowed. He's always on th' level an' he's always jes' th' same as yeh see 'im now--
bla
glp!
bla
bla
THE NEXT ROUND IS ON ME BOYS!!
Oh! No, no no Drippy!
Some other time!
It's my turn now!
T'night yer our guest!

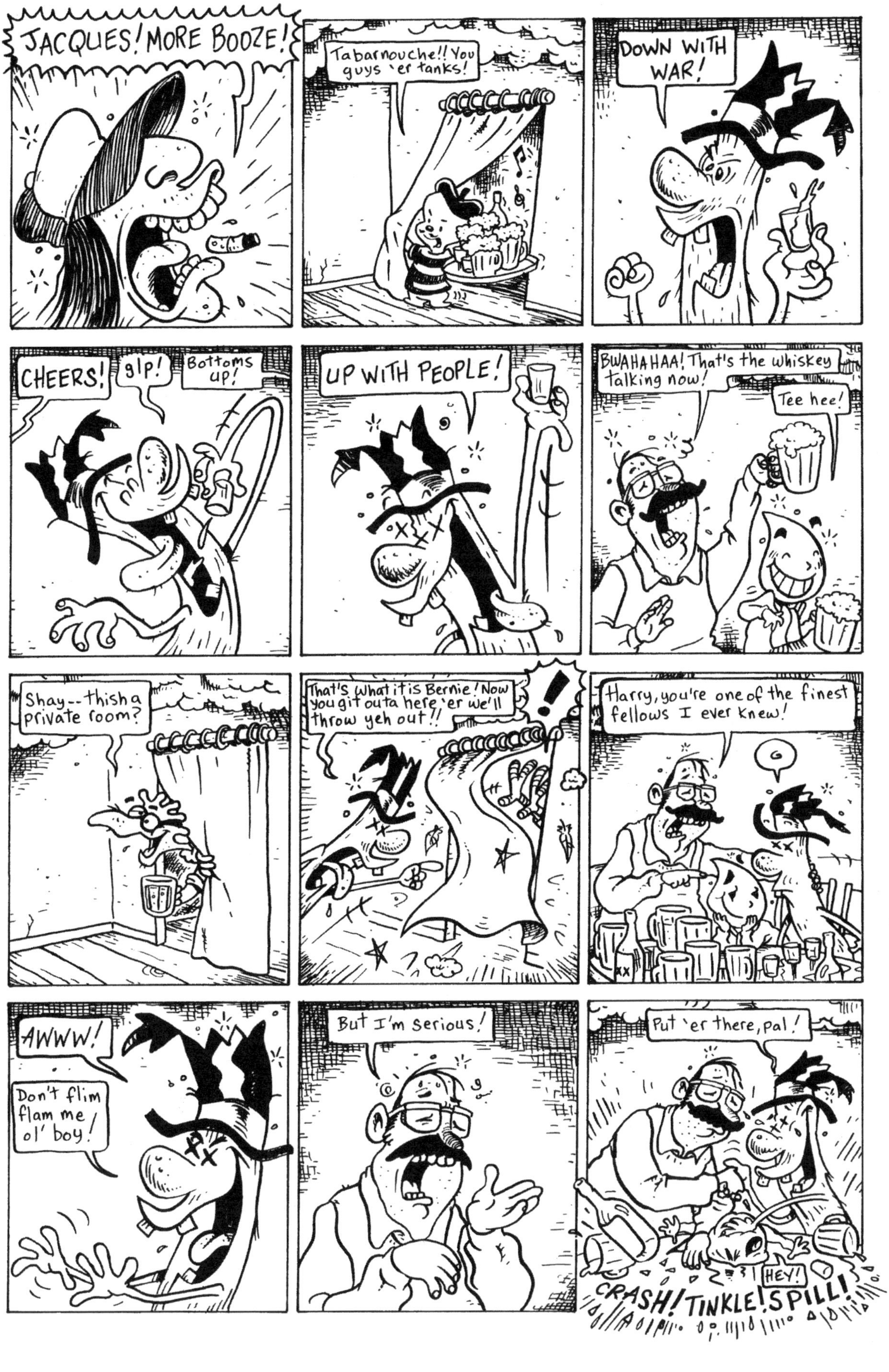
JACQUES! MORE BOOZE!
Tabarnouche!! You guys 'er tanks!
DOWN WITH WAR!
CHEERS!
glp!
Bottoms up!
UP WITH PEOPLE!
BWAHAHAA! That's the whiskey talking now!
Tee hee!
Shay--thisha private room?
That's what it is Bernie! Now you git outa here 'er we'll throw yeh out!!
!
Harry, you're one of the finest fellows I ever knew!
AWWW!
Don't flim flam me ol' boy!
But I'm serious!
Put 'er there, pal!
HEY!
CRASH! TINKLE! SPILL!

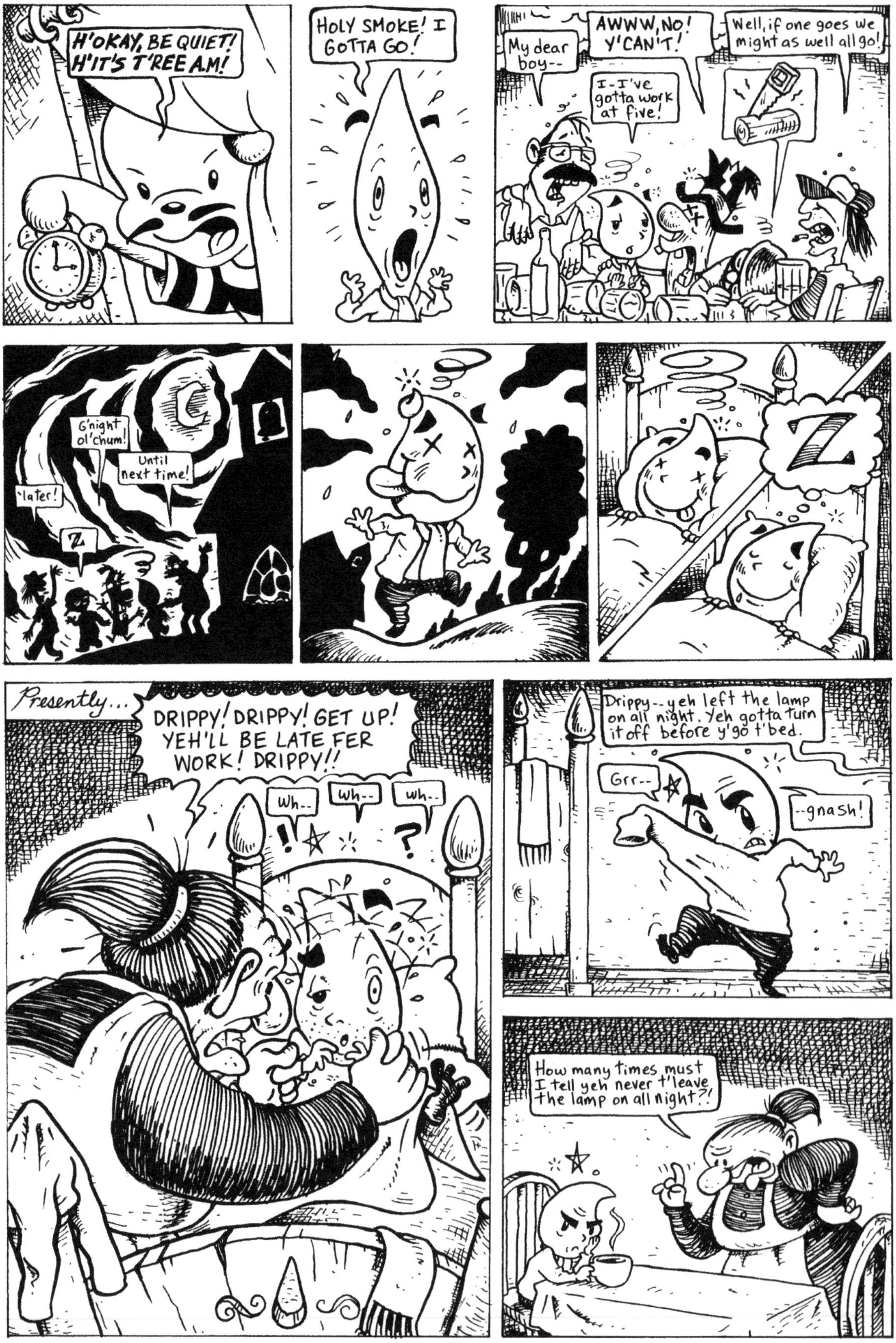

H'OKAY, BE QUIET! H'IT'S T'REE A.M!
HOLY SMOKE! I GOTTA GO!
My dear boy--
AWWW, NO! Y'CAN'T!
I-I've gotta work at five!
Well, if one goes we might as well all go!
G'night ol'chum!
Until next time!
'later!
Z
Z
Presently...
DRIPPY! DRIPPY! GET UP! YEH'LL BE LATE FER WORK! DRIPPY!!
Wh--
Wh--
Wh--
Drippy--yeh left the lamp on all night. Yeh gotta turn it off before y'go t'bed.
Grr--
--gnash!
How many times must I tell yeh never t'leave the lamp on all night?!

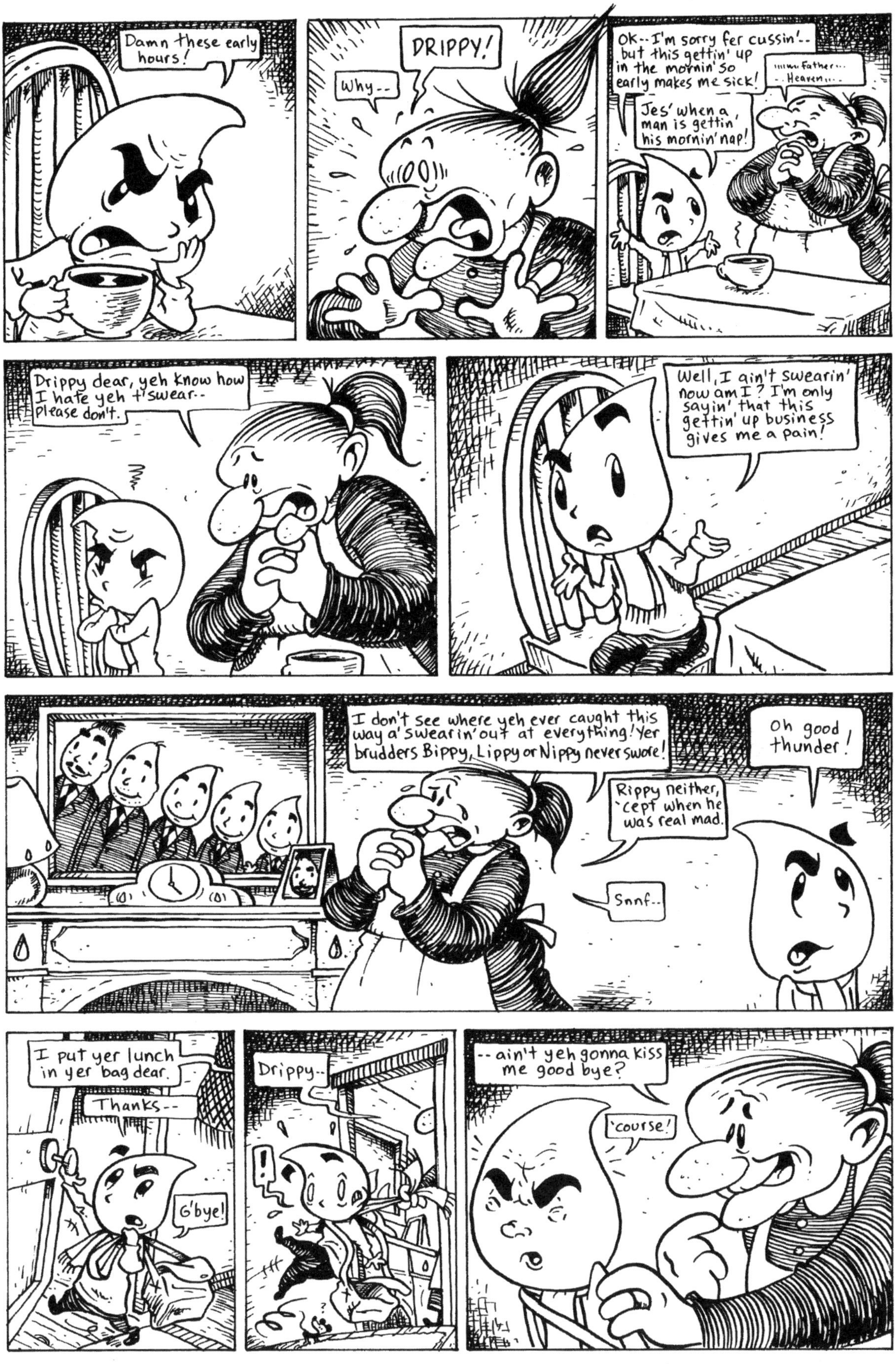

Damn these early hours!
DRIPPY!
Why--
OK--I'm sorry fer cussin'--but this gettin' up in the mornin' so early makes me sick!
Jes' when a man is gettin' his mornin' nap!
.....Father... --Heaven....
Drippy dear, yeh know how I hate yeh t'swear--Please don't.
Well, I ain't swearin' now am I? I'm only sayin' that this gettin' up business gives me a pain!
I don't see where yeh ever caught this way a'swearin'out at everything! Yer brudders Bippy, Lippy or Nippy never swore!
Rippy neither, 'cept when he was real mad.
Snnf--
Oh good thunder!
I put yer lunch in yer bag dear.
Thanks--
G'bye!
Drippy--
--ain't yeh gonna kiss me good bye?
'course!

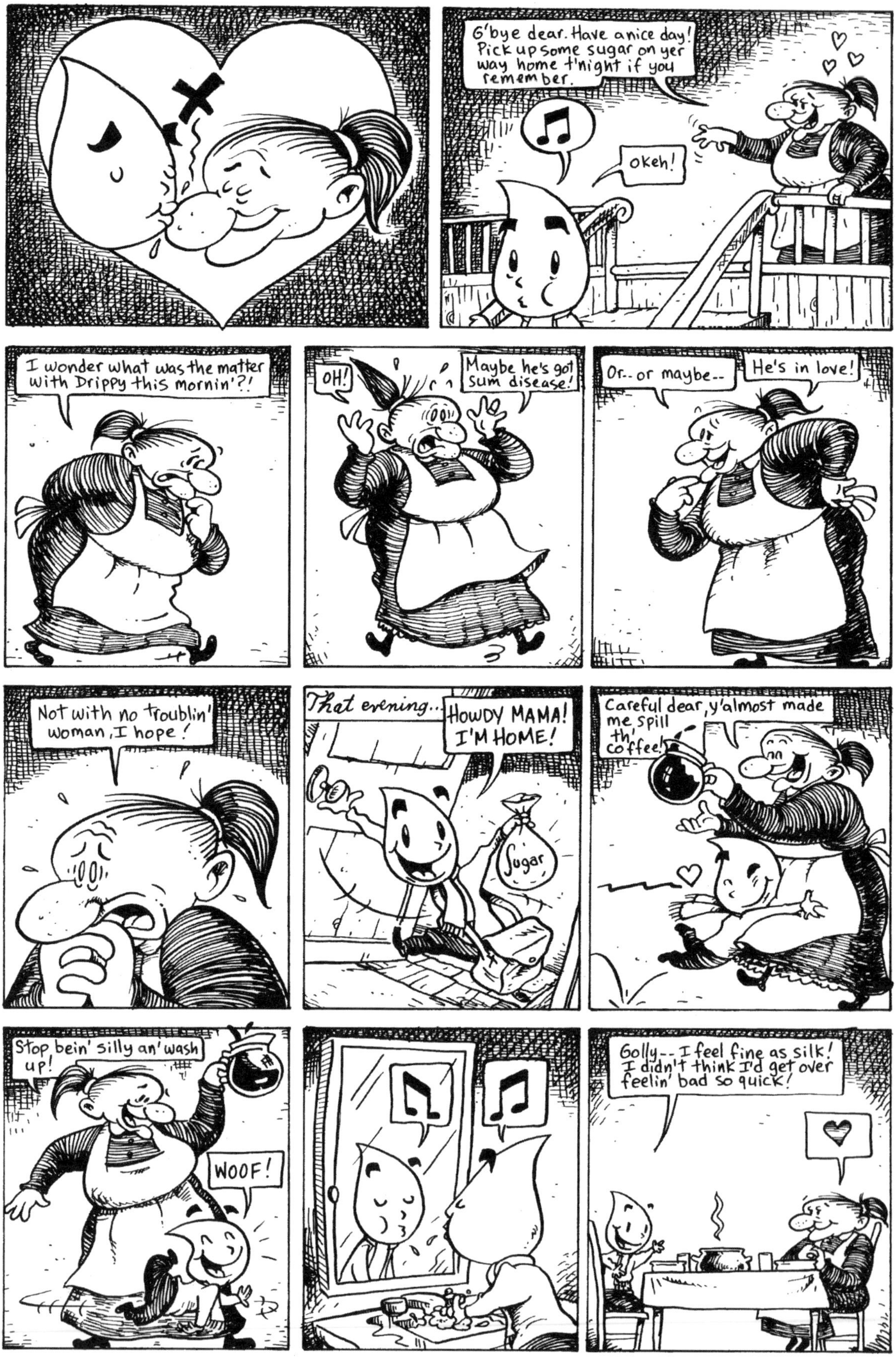
G'bye dear. Have a nice day! Pick up some sugar on yer way home t'night if you remember.
Okeh!
I wonder what was the matter with Drippy this mornin'?!
OH!
Maybe he's got sum disease!
Or.. or maybe..
He's in love!
Not with no troublin' woman, I hope!
That evening...
HOWDY MAMA! I'M HOME!
Sugar
Careful dear, y'almost made me spill th' coffee!
Stop bein' silly an' wash up!
WOOF!
Golly -- I feel fine as silk! I didn't think I'd get over feelin' bad so quick!

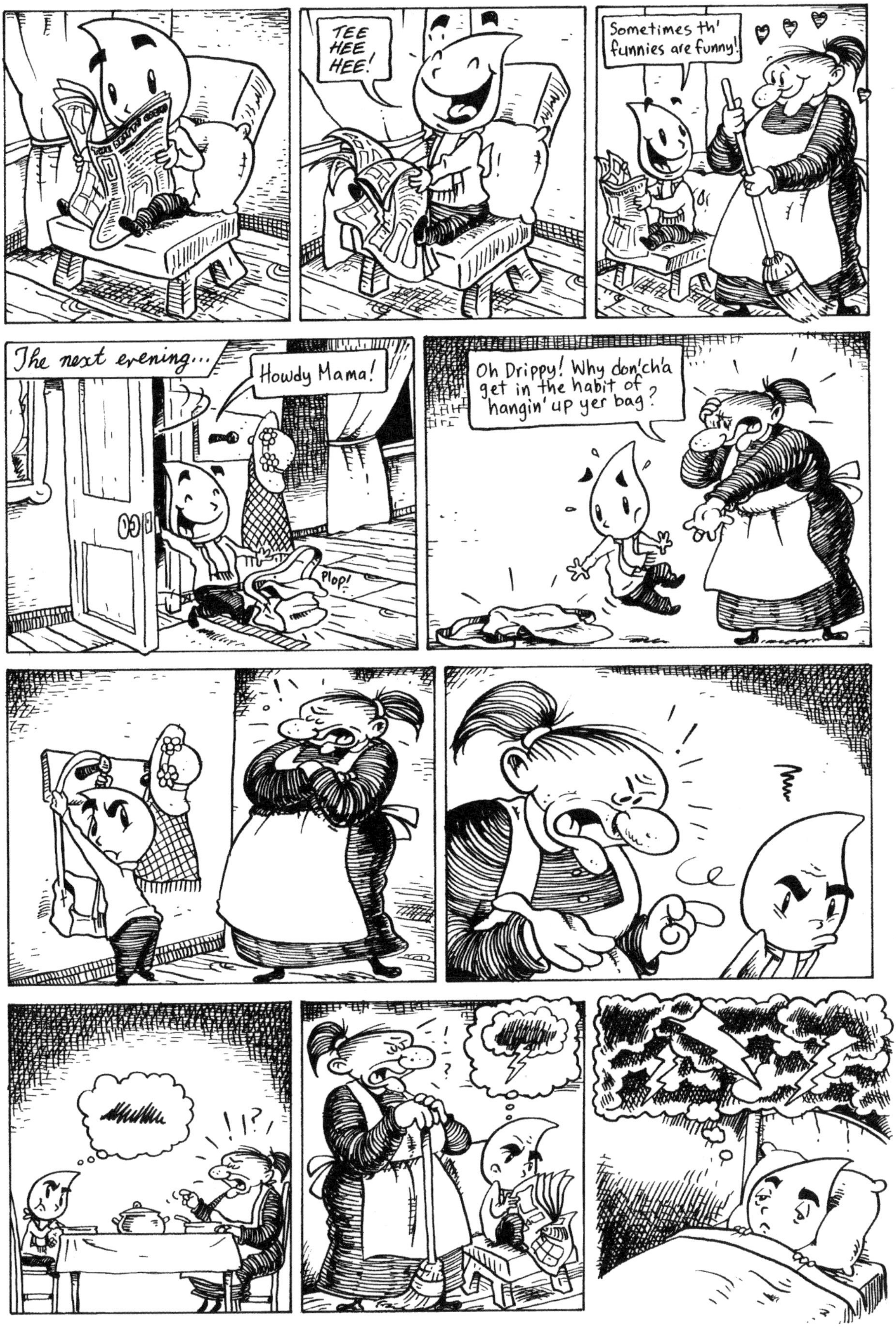
TEE HEE HEE!
Sometimes th' funnies are funny!
The next evening...
Howdy Mama!
Plop!
Oh Drippy! Why don'ch'a get in the habit of hangin' up yer bag?

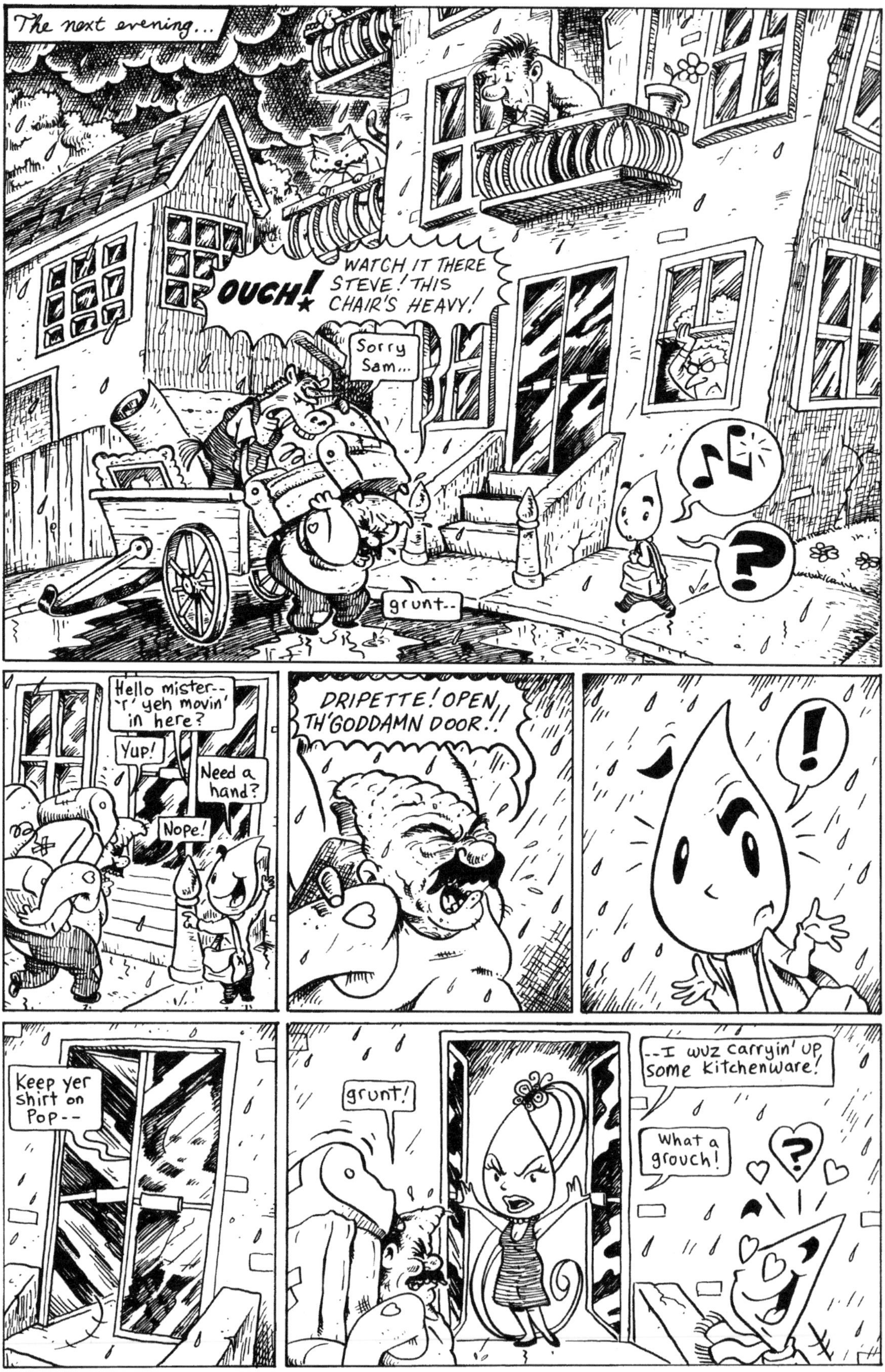

The next evening...
OUCH!
WATCH IT THERE STEVE! THIS CHAIR'S HEAVY!
Sorry Sam...
grunt--
?
Hello mister-- 'r' yeh movin' in here?
Yup!
Need a hand?
Nope!
DRIPETTE! OPEN TH'GODDAMN DOOR!!
!
Keep yer shirt on Pop--
grunt!
--I wuz carryin' up some kitchenware!
What a grouch!
?

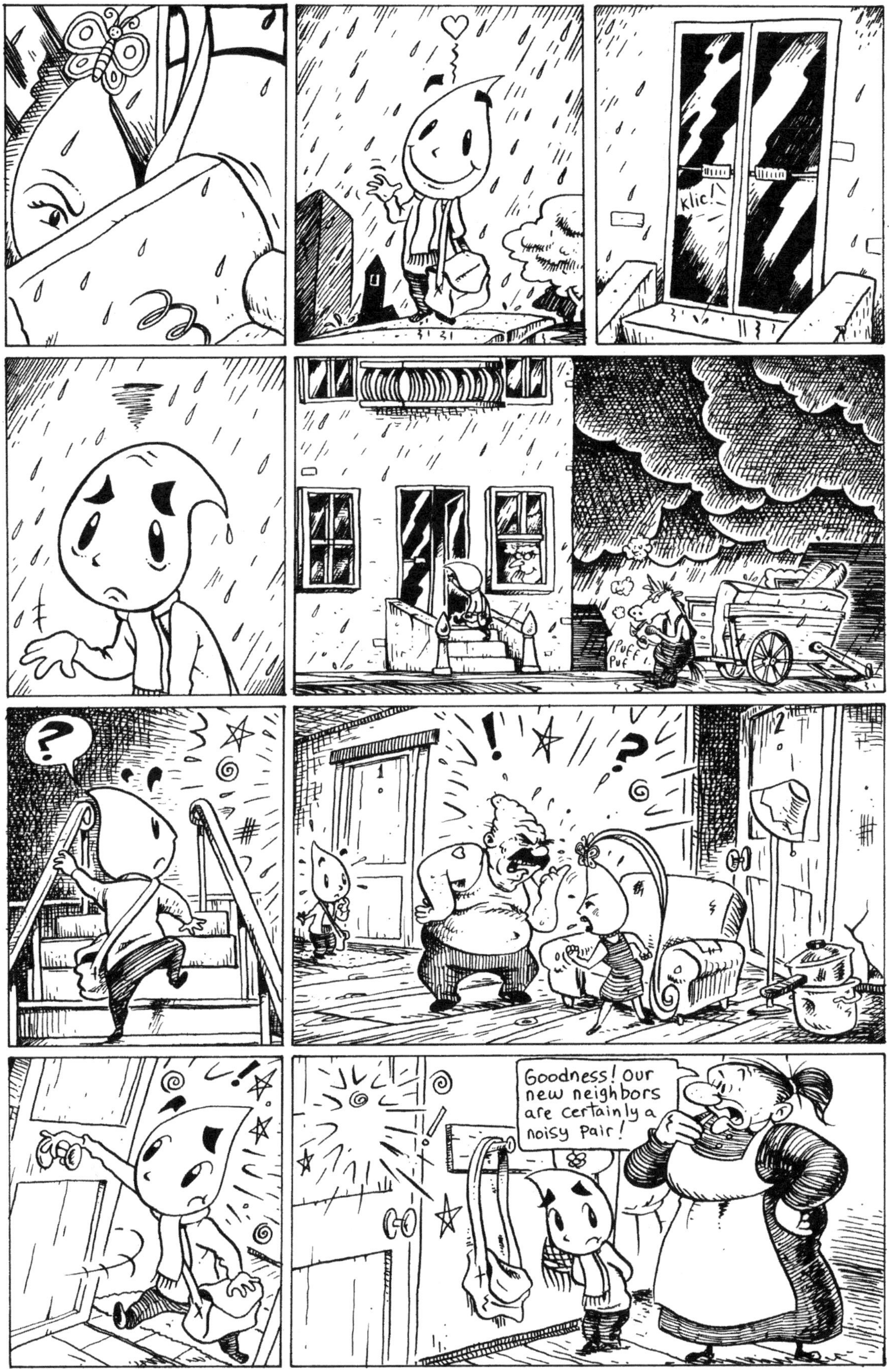
klic!
Puff
Puf
Goodness! Our new neighbors are certainly a noisy pair!

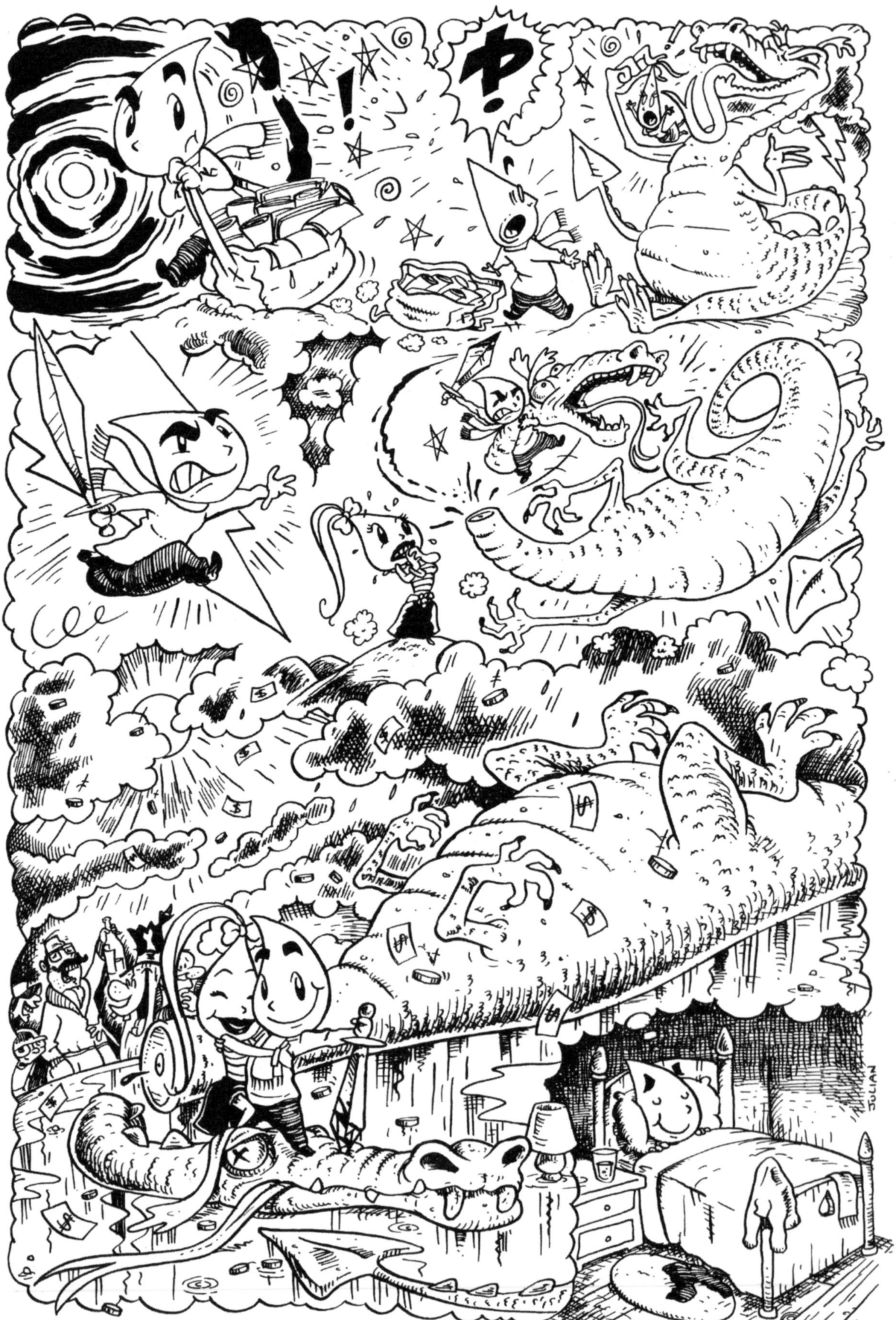
JULIAN

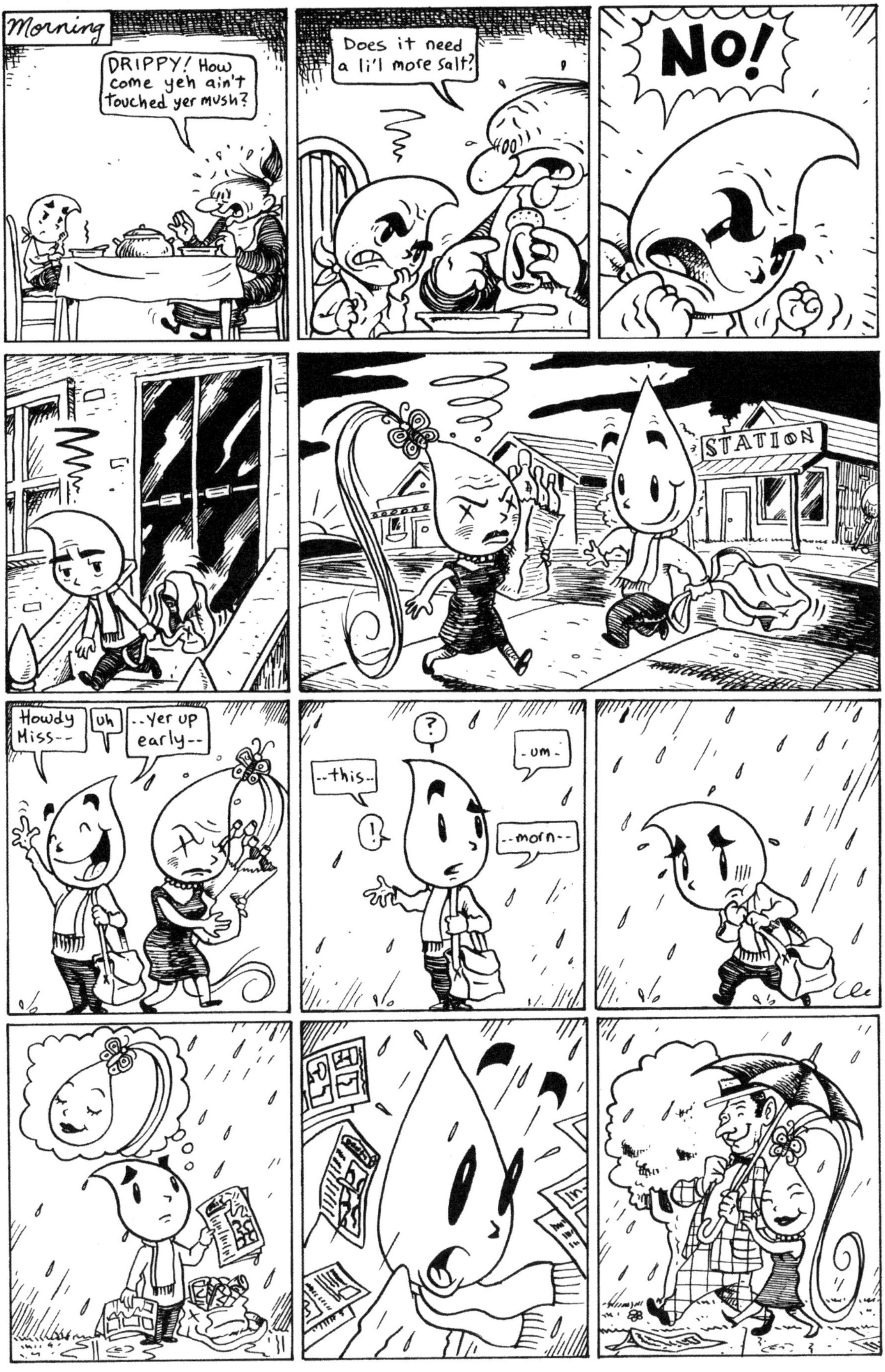
Morning
DRIPPY! How come yeh ain't touched yer mush?
Does it need a li'l more salt?
NO!
STATION
Howdy Miss--
uh
..yer up early--
?
--this--
!
-um-
--morn--

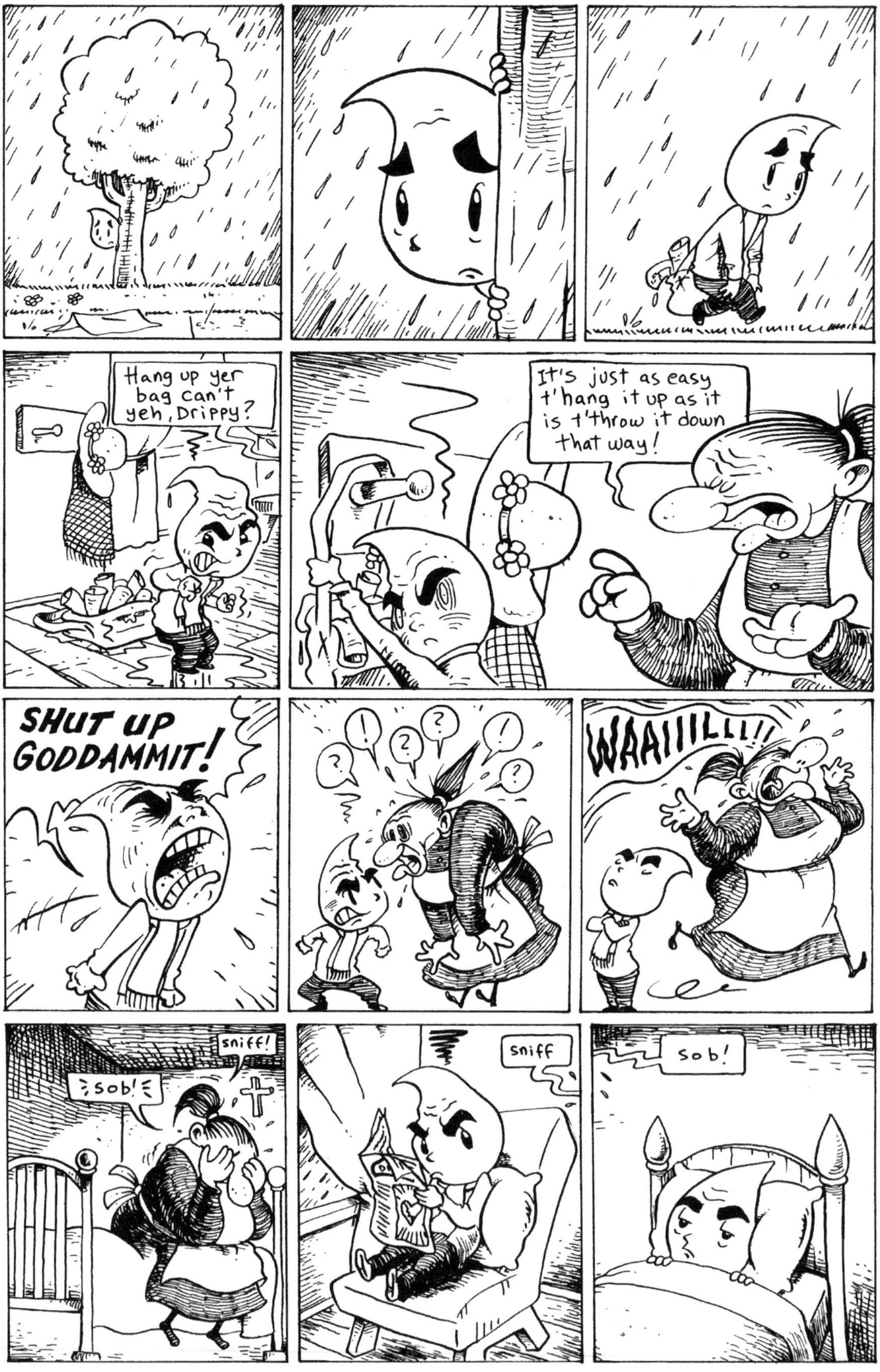
Hang up yer bag can't yeh, Drippy?
It's just as easy t'hang it up as it is t'throw it down that way!
SHUT UP GODDAMMIT!
?
!
?
?
!
?
WAAIIILLL!!
sniff!
sob!
sniff
sob!

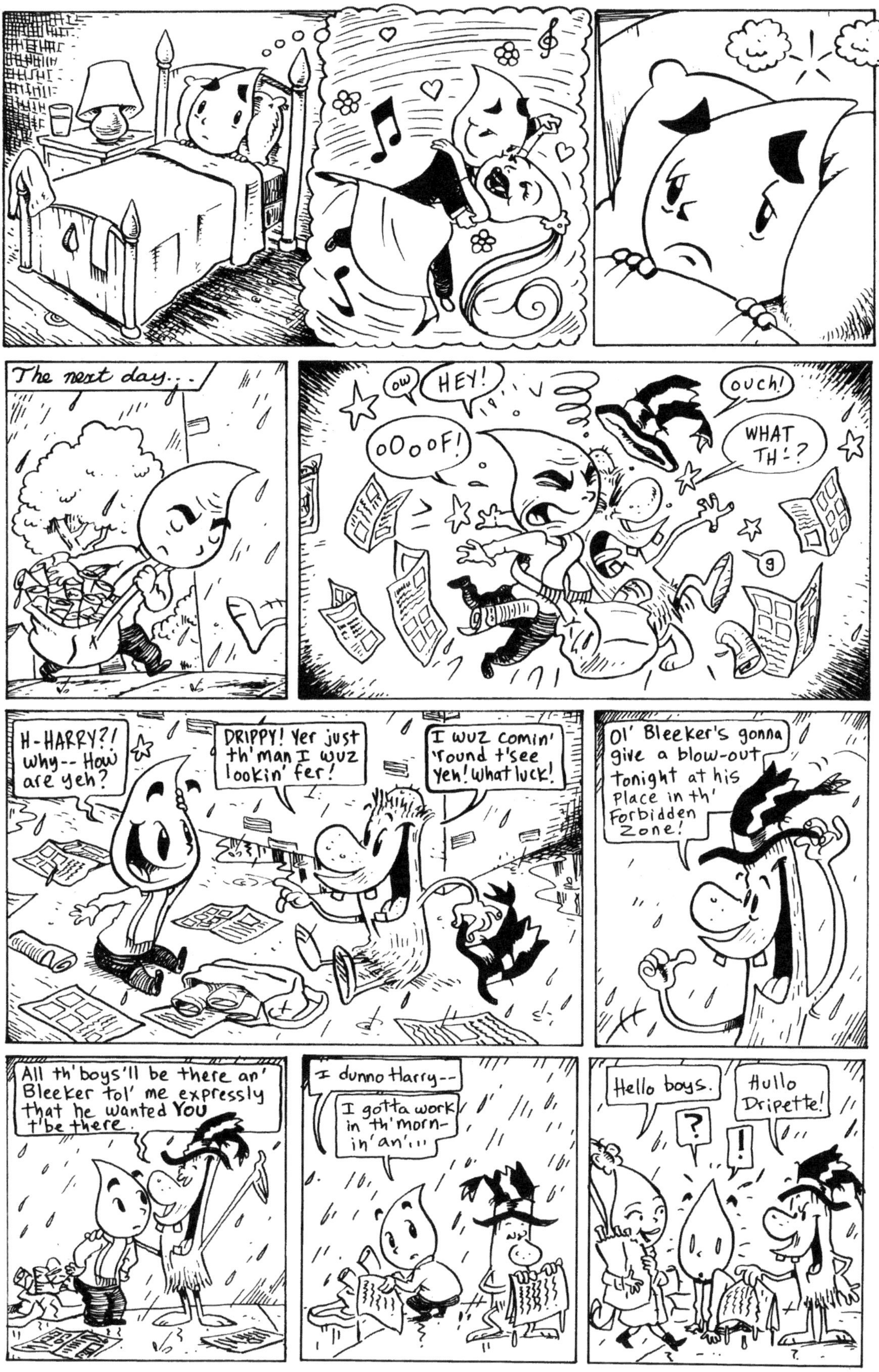

The next day...
ow
HEY!
ouch!
OOOOF!
WHAT TH-?
H-HARRY?! why-- How are yeh?
DRIPPY! Yer just th'man I wuz lookin' fer!
I wuz comin' 'round t'see yeh! what luck!
Ol' Bleeker's gonna give a blow-out tonight at his place in th' Forbidden Zone!
All th'boys'll be there an' Bleeker tol' me expressly that he wanted YOU t'be there.
I dunno Harry--
I gotta work in th'morn-in'an'...
Hello boys.
Hullo Dripette!
?
!

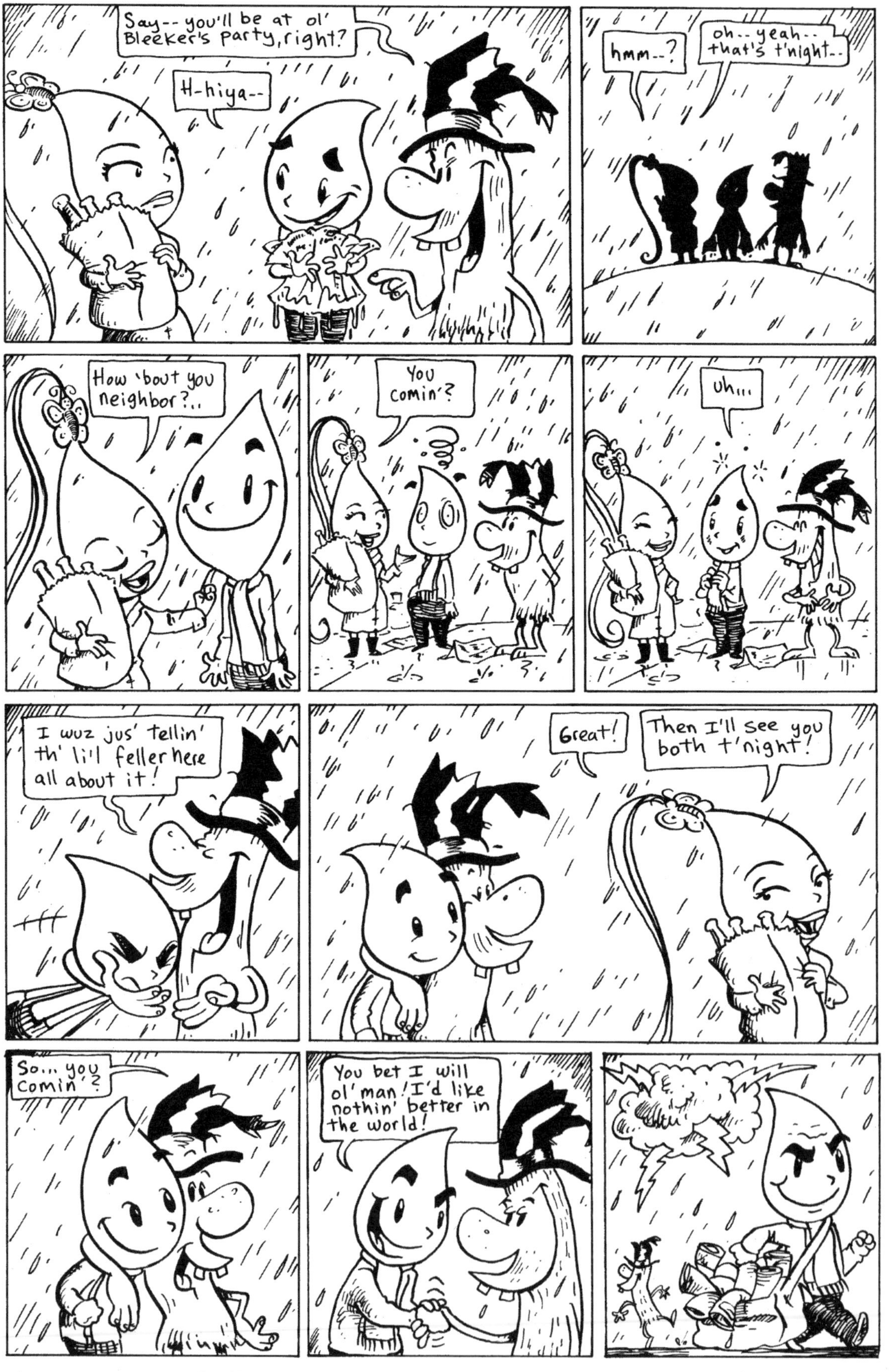
Say-- you'll be at ol' Bleeker's party, right?
H-hiya--
hmm--?
oh-- yeah-- that's t'night--
How 'bout you neighbor?..
You comin'?
Uh...
I wuz jus' tellin' th' li'l feller here all about it!
Great!
Then I'll see you both t'night!
So... you comin'?
You bet I will ol' man! I'd like nothin' better in the world!

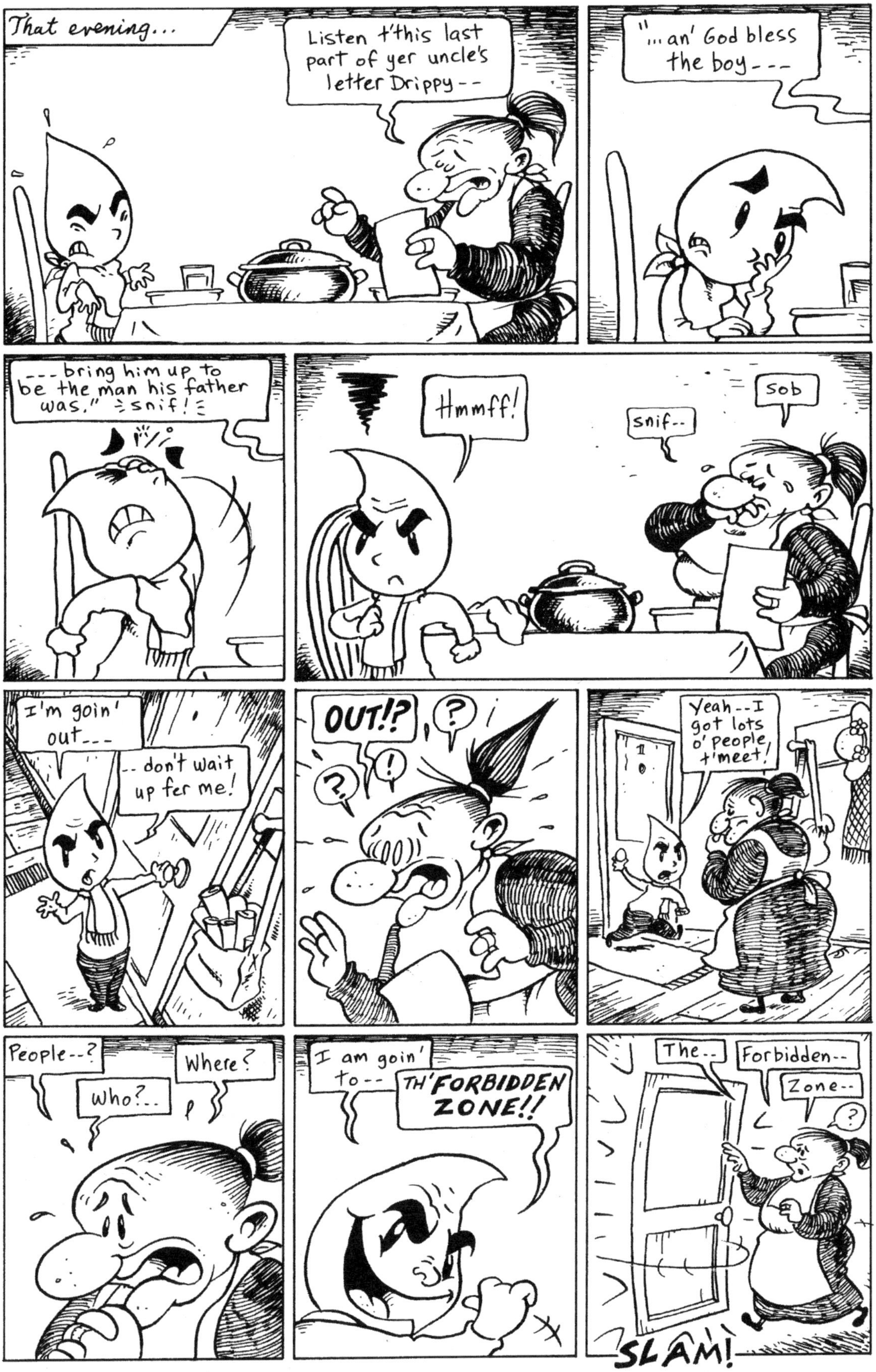

That evening...
Listen t'this last part of yer uncle's letter Drippy--
"...an' God bless the boy---
---bring him up to be the man his father was." snif!
Hmmff!
snif--
sob
I'm goin' out---
--don't wait up fer me!
OUT!?
?
!
?
Yeah--I got lots o' people t'meet!
People--?
Who?..
Where?
I am goin' to--
TH' FORBIDDEN ZONE!!
The--
Forbidden--
Zone--
?
SLAM!

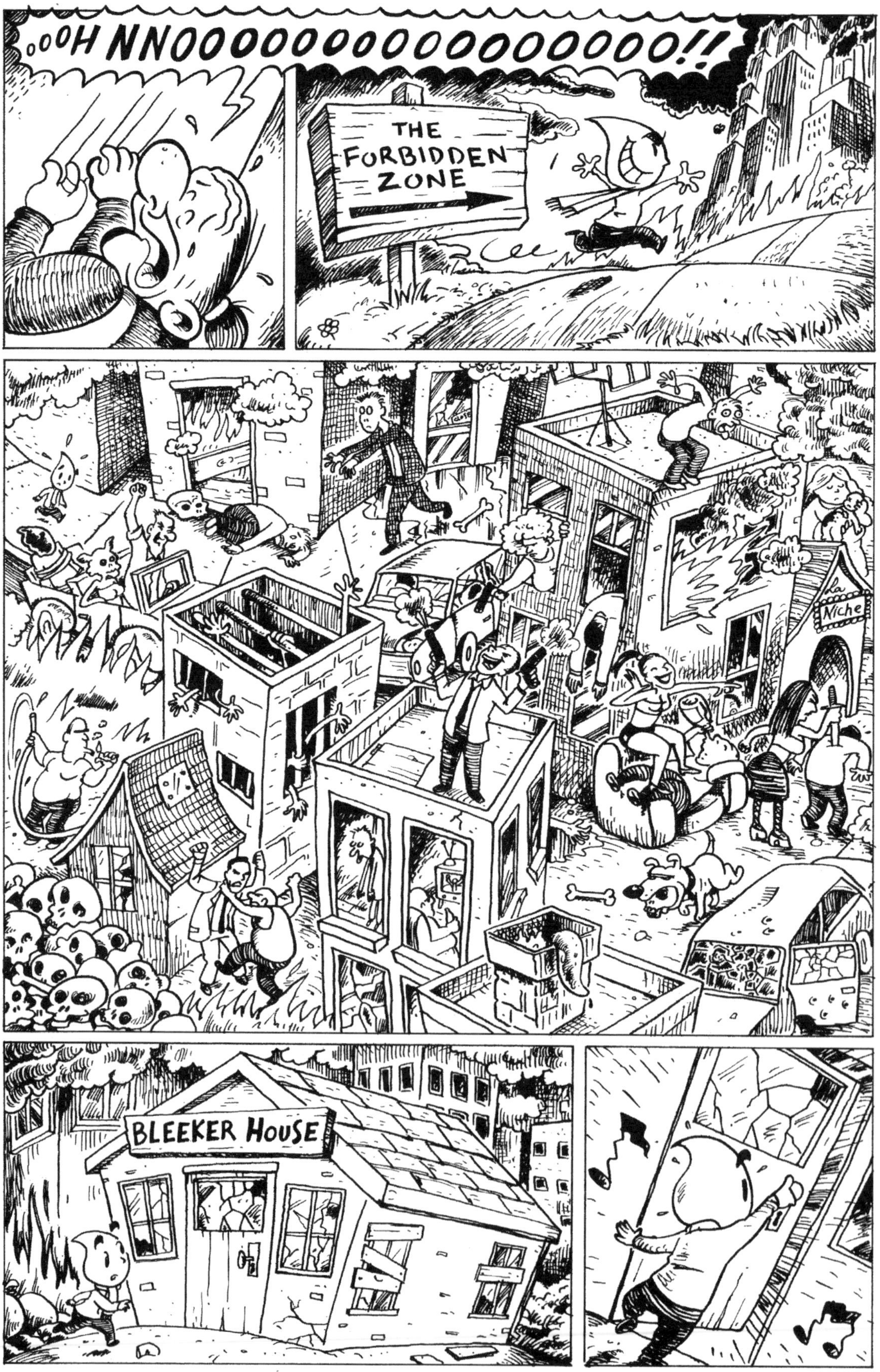
oooH NNOOOOOOOOOOOOOOOO!!
THE FORBIDDEN ZONE
La Niche
BLEEKER HOUSE

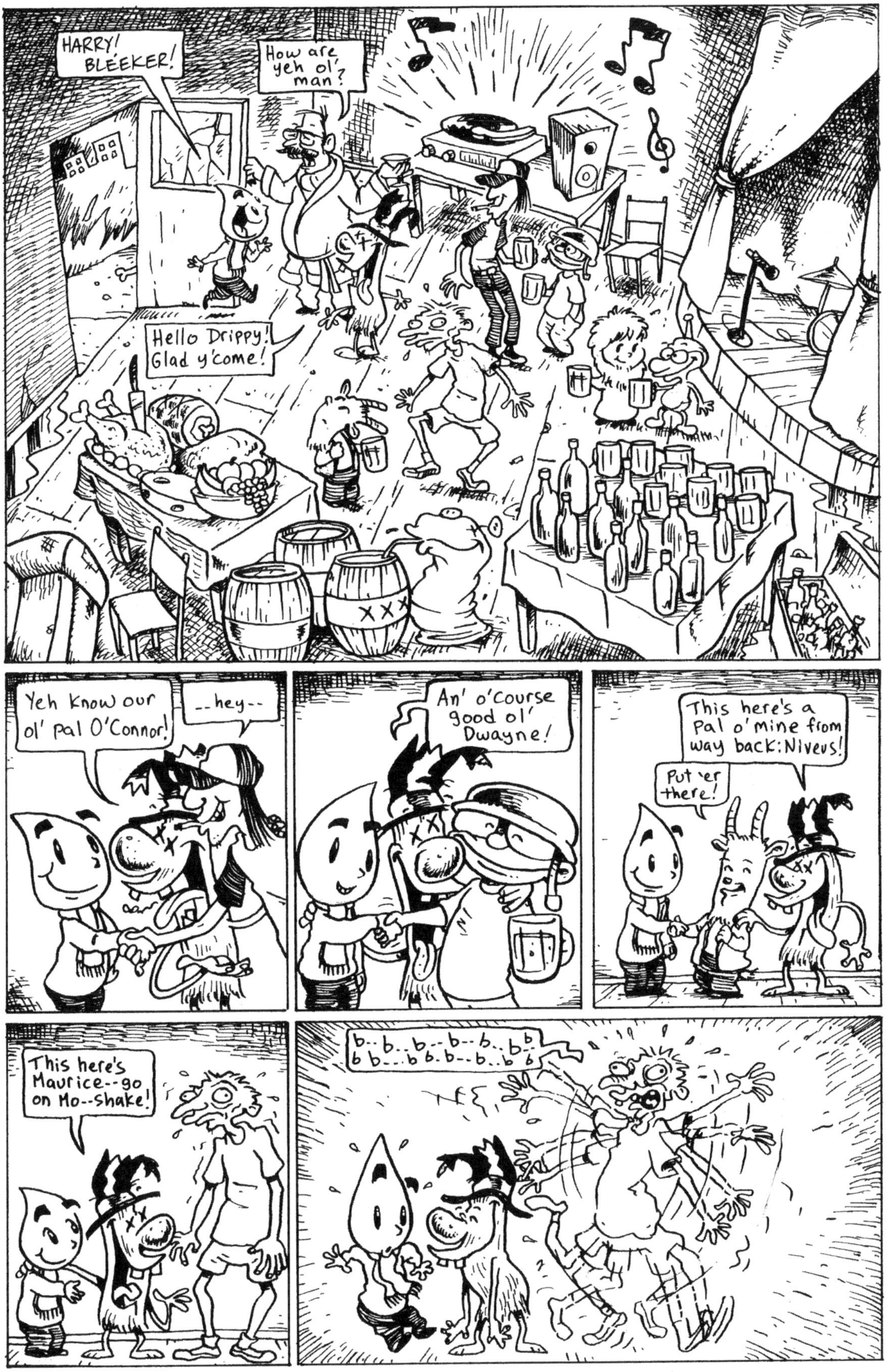
HARRY! BLEEKER!
How are yeh ol' man?
Hello Drippy! Glad y'come!
Yeh know our ol' pal O'Connor!
--hey--
An' o'course good ol' Dwayne!
This here's a pal o'mine from way back: Niveus!
Put 'er there!
This here's Maurice--go on Mo--shake!
b..b..b..b..b..b..b b b...b b.b..b..b..b b

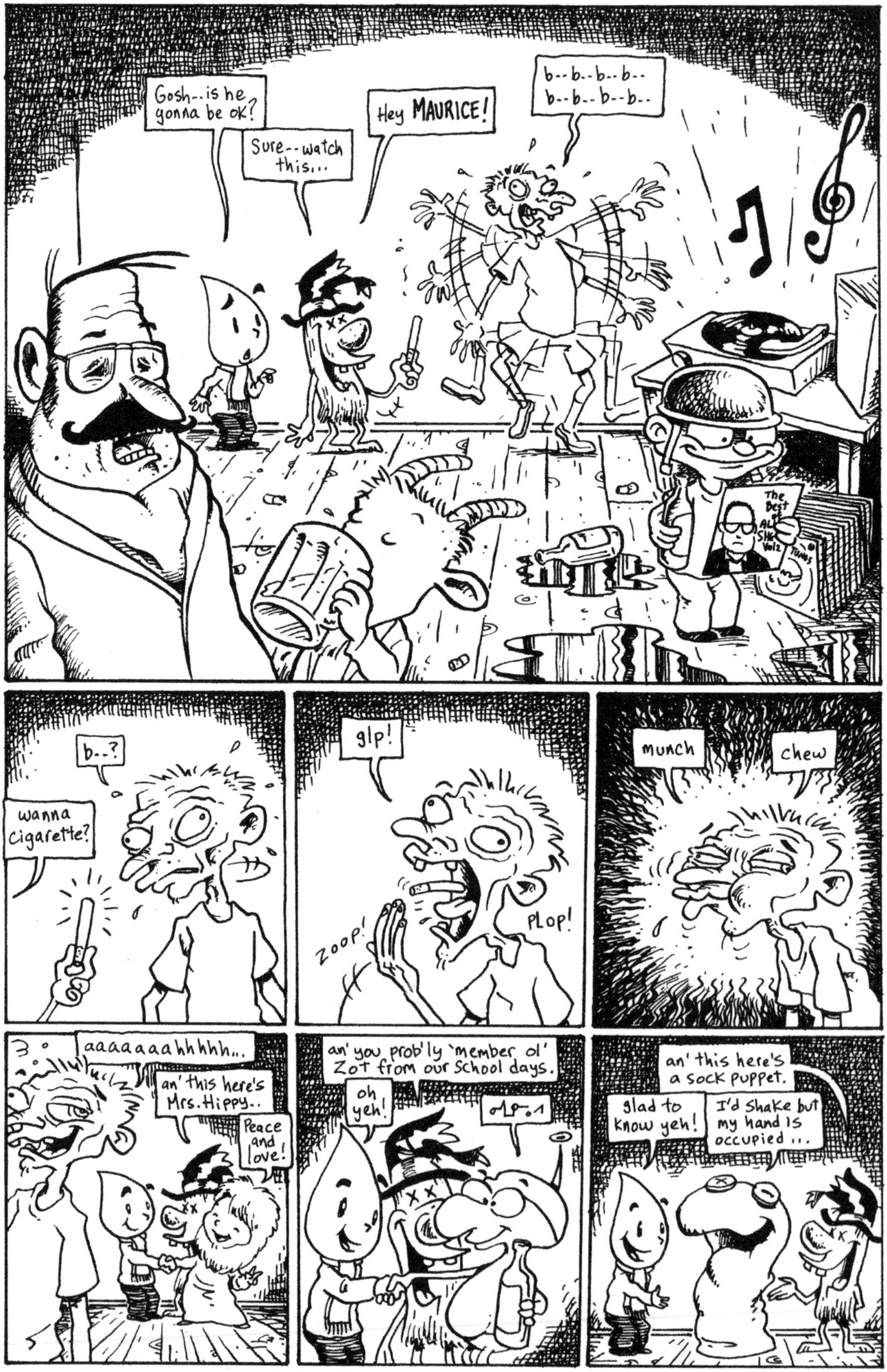

Gosh--is he gonna be OK?
Sure--watch this...
Hey MAURICE!
b--b--b--b--
b--b--b--b--
The Best of AL SHE Vol 2
b--?
wanna cigarette?
glp!
ZOOP!
PLOP!
munch
chew
aaaaaaahhhhh...
an' this here's Mrs. Hippy..
Peace and love!
an' you prob'ly 'member ol' Zot from our School days.
oh yeh!
glad to know yeh!
an' this here's a sock puppet.
I'd shake but my hand is occupied...

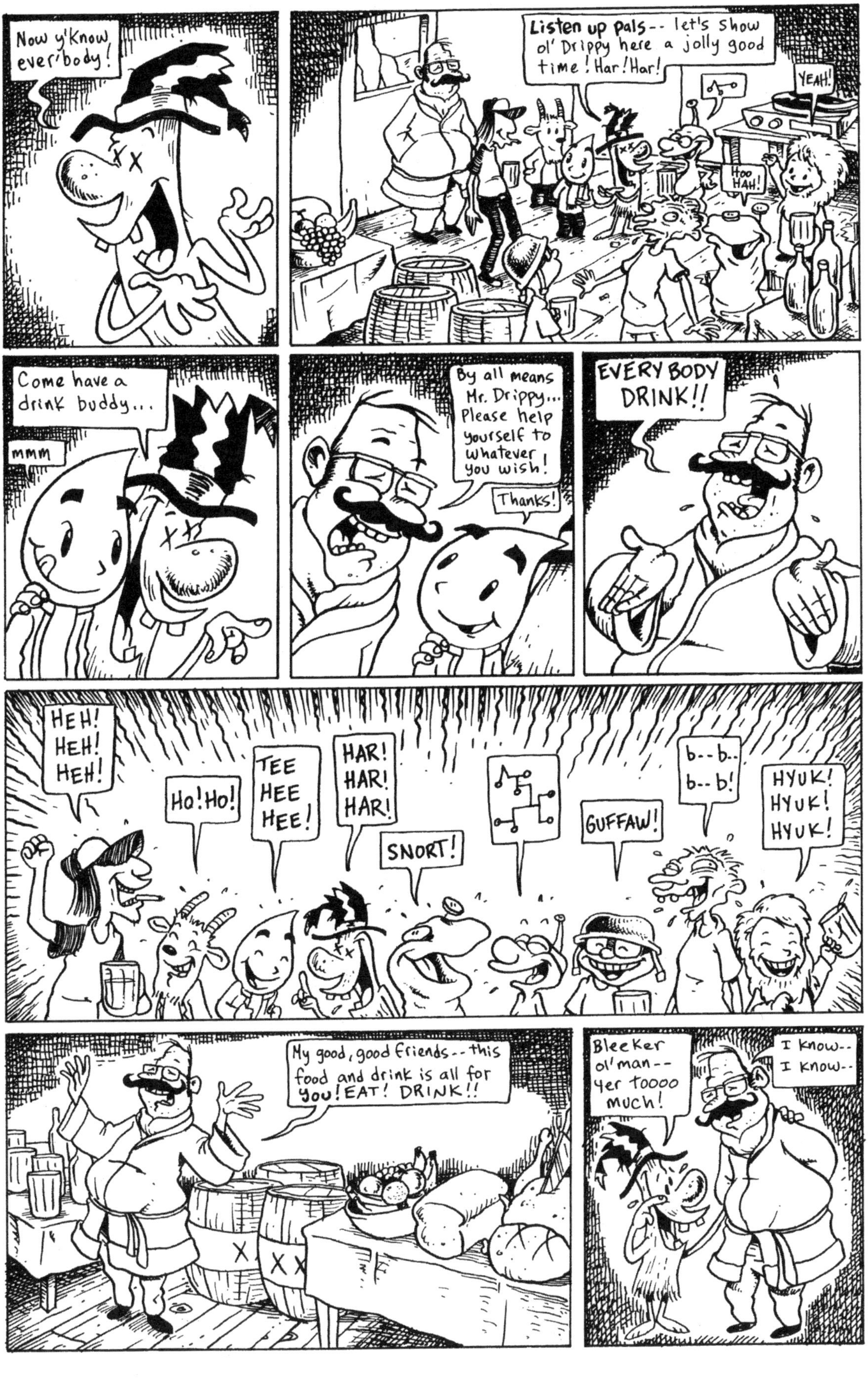
Now y'know ever'body!
Listen up pals-- let's show ol' Drippy here a jolly good time! Har! Har!
YEAH!
HOO HAH!
Come have a drink buddy...
mmm
By all means Mr. Drippy... Please help yourself to whatever you wish!
Thanks!
EVERY BODY DRINK!!
HEH! HEH! HEH!
Ho! Ho!
TEE HEE HEE!
HAR! HAR! HAR!
SNORT!
GUFFAW!
b-- b.. b-- b!
HYUK! HYUK! HYUK!
My good, good friends-- this food and drink is all for you! EAT! DRINK!!
Bleeker ol' man-- yer toooo much!
I know-- I know--

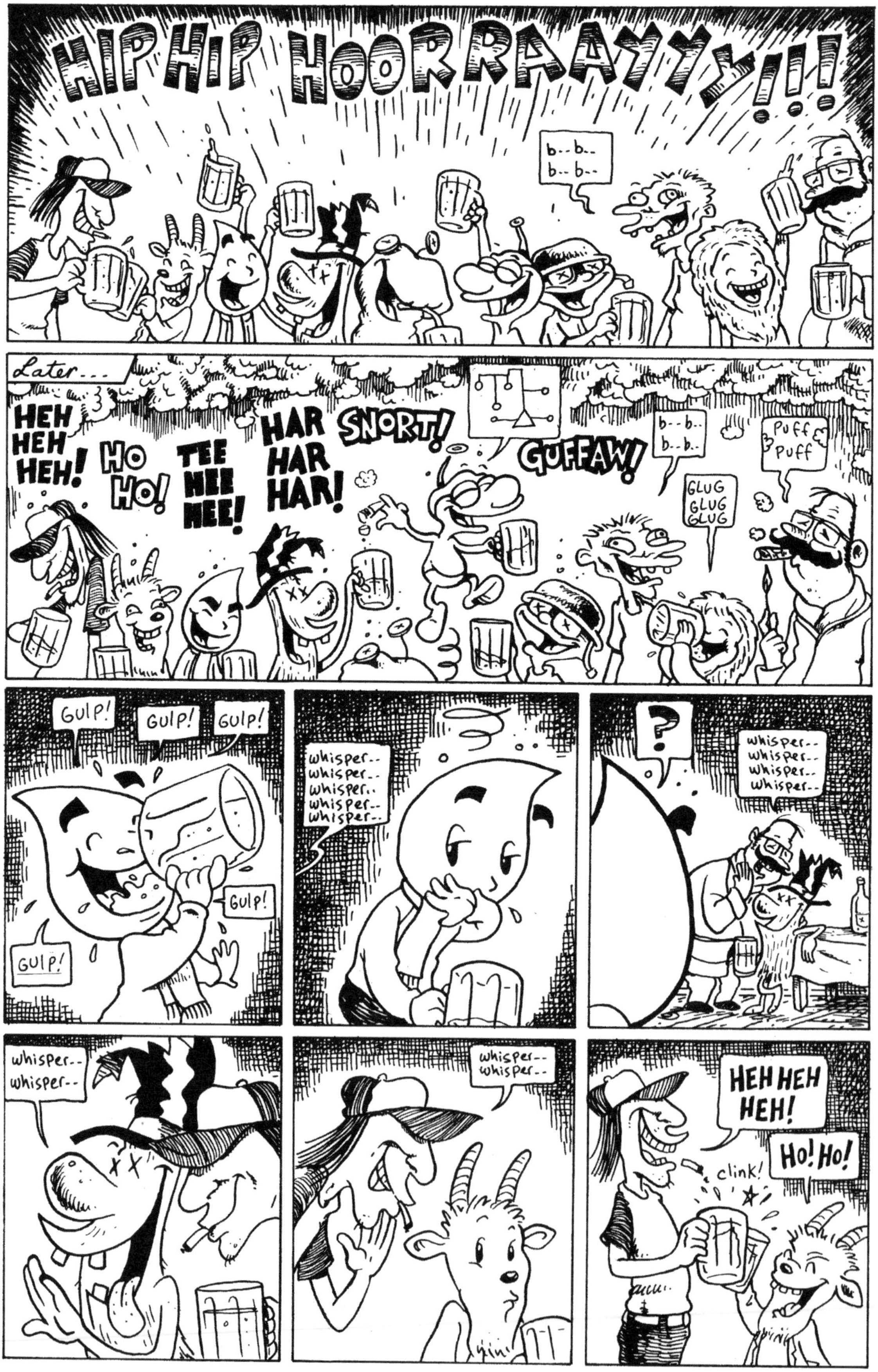
HIP HIP HOORRAAYYY!!!
b-- b--
b-- b--
Later...
HEH HEH HEH!
HO HO!
TEE HEE HEE!
HAR HAR HAR!
SNORT!
GUFFAW!
b-- b--
b-- b--
Puff Puff
GLUG GLUG GLUG
GULP!
GULP!
GULP!
GULP!
GULP!
whisper--
whisper--
whisper--
whisper--
whisper--
?
whisper--
whisper--
whisper--
whisper--
whisper--
whisper--
whisper--
whisper--
HEH HEH HEH!
clink!
Ho! Ho!

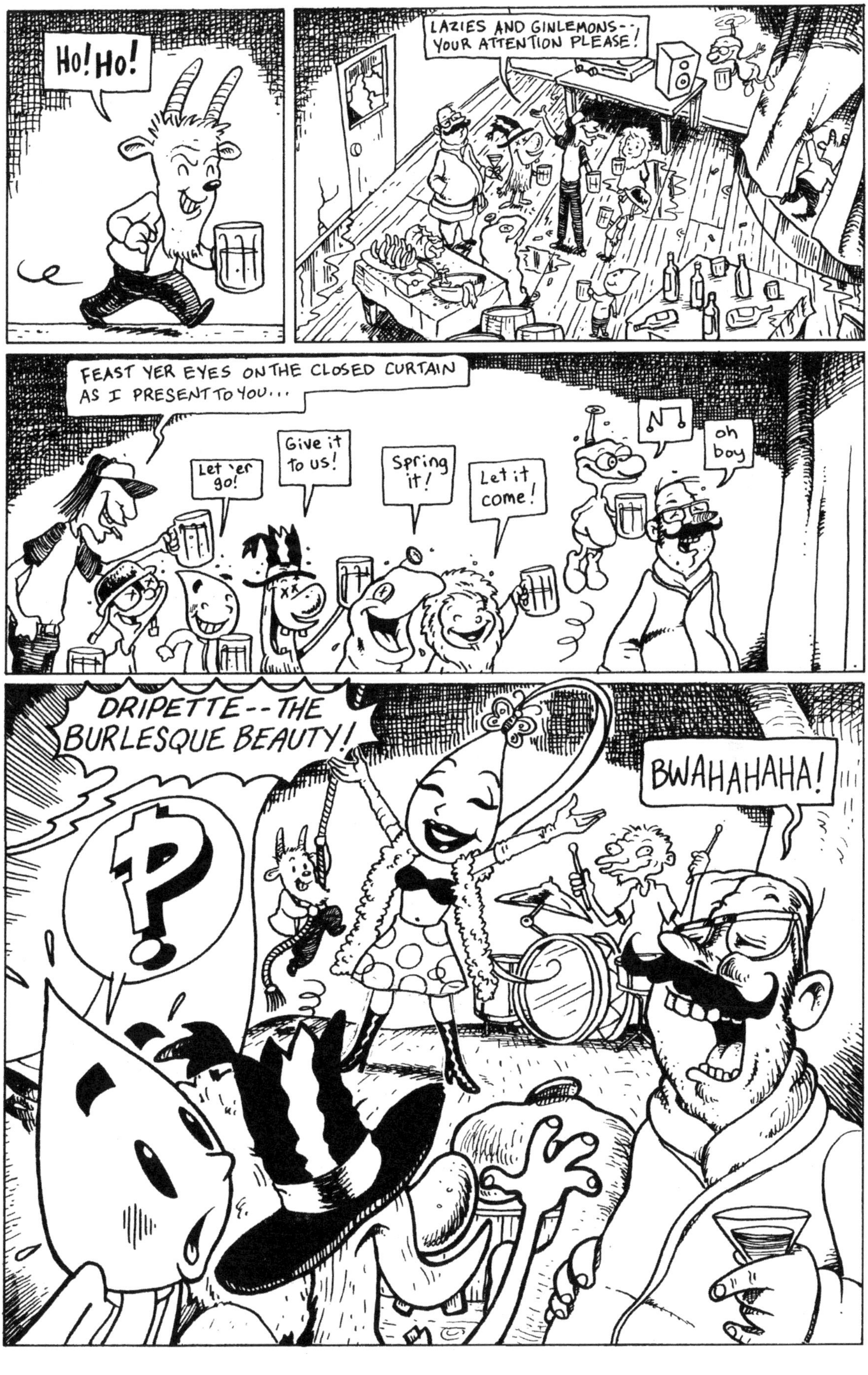

HO! HO!
LAZIES AND GINLEMONS--
YOUR ATTENTION PLEASE!
FEAST YER EYES ON THE CLOSED CURTAIN
AS I PRESENT TO YOU...
Let 'er go!
Give it to us!
Spring it!
Let it come!
oh boy
DRIPETTE--THE
BURLESQUE BEAUTY!
BWAHAHAHA!

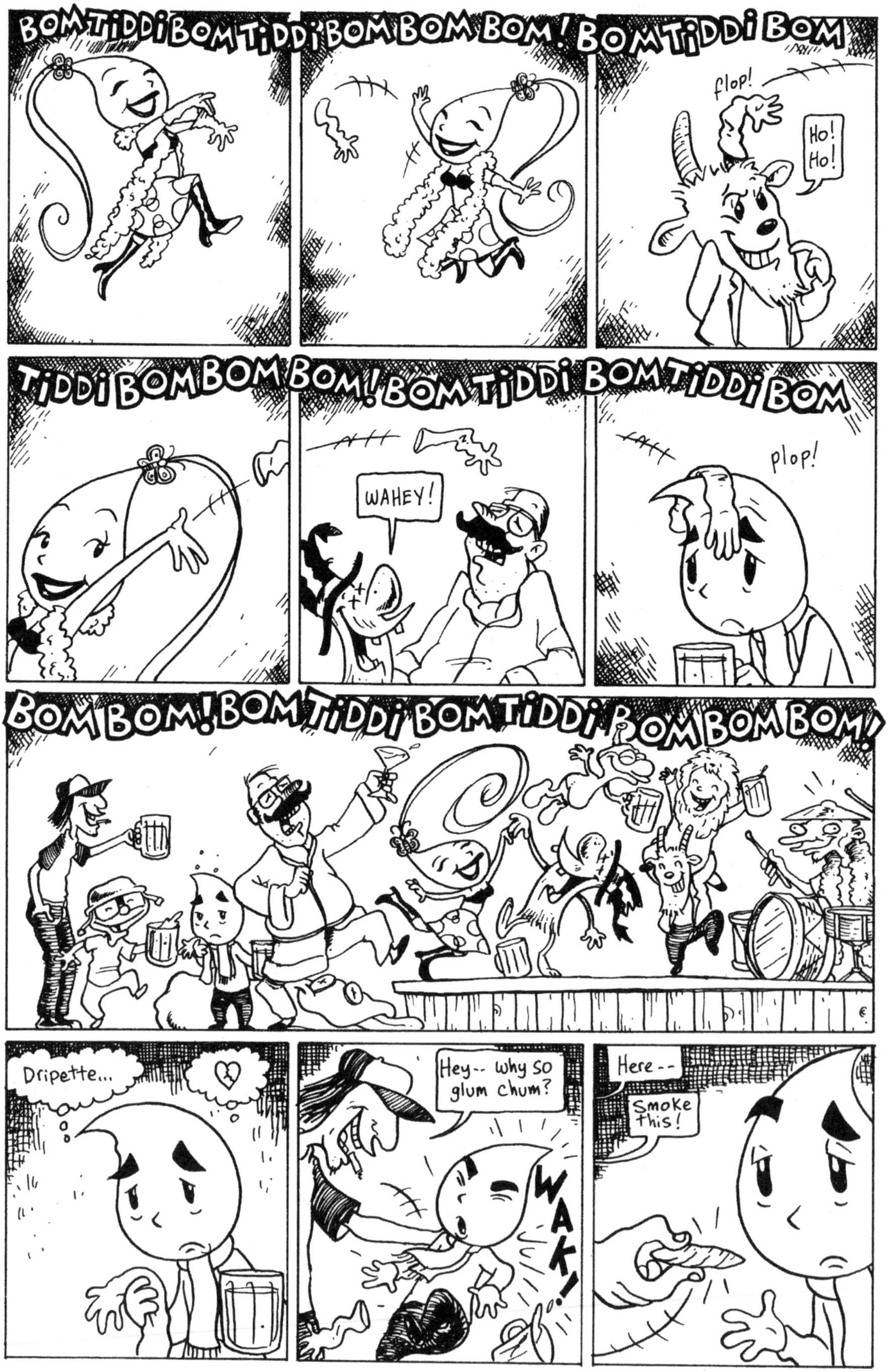
BOM TIDDI BOM TIDDI BOM BOM BOM! BOM TIDDI BOM
flop!
Ho! Ho!
TIDDI BOM BOM BOM! BOM TIDDI BOM TIDDI BOM
WAHEY!
plop!
BOM BOM! BOM TIDDI BOM TIDDI BOM BOM BOM!
Dripette...
Hey-- why so glum chum?
WAK!
Here--
Smoke this!

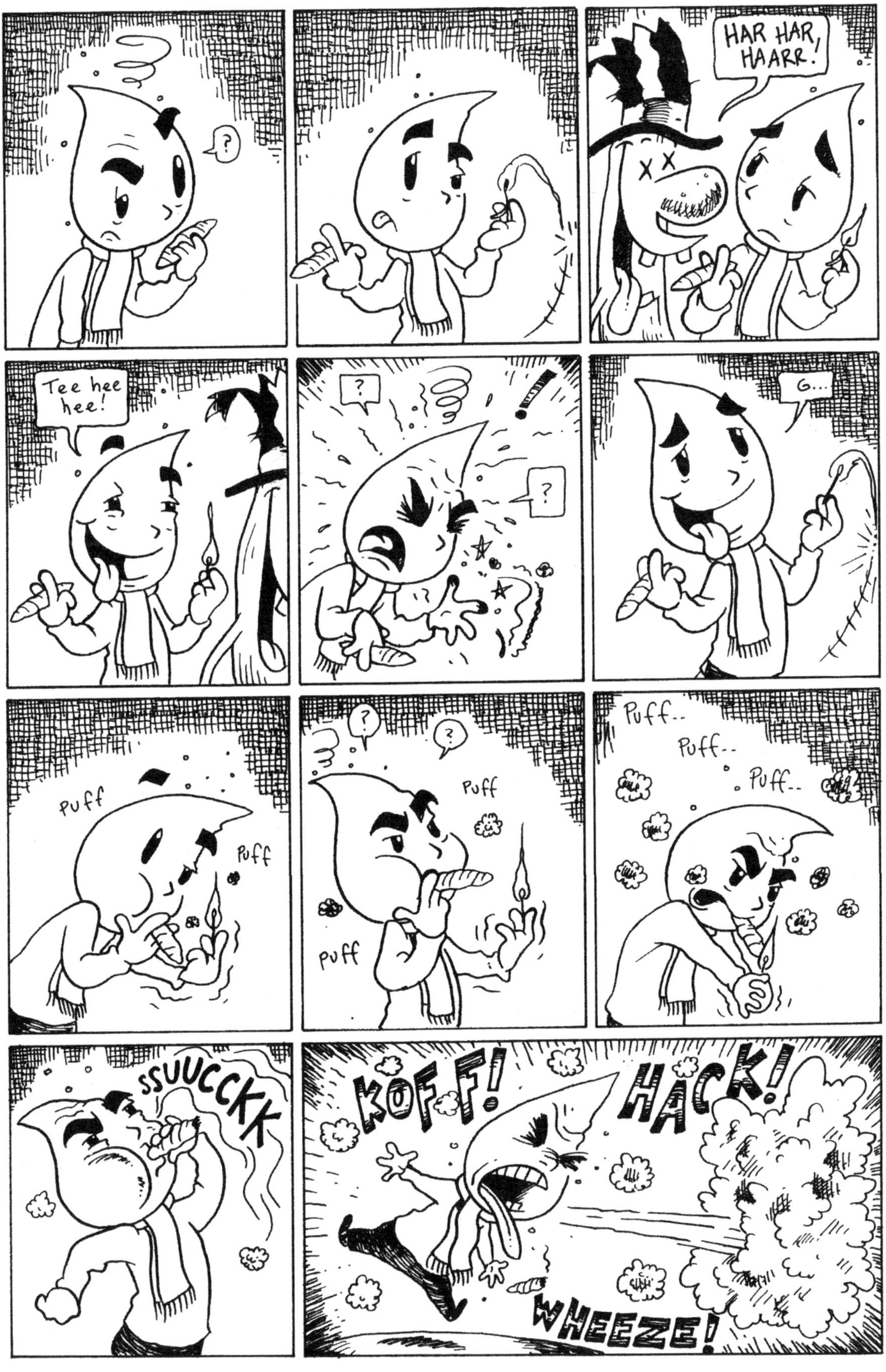

?
HAR HAR, HAARR!
Tee hee hee!
?
!
?
G...
Puff
Puff
?
?
Puff
Puff
Puff--
Puff--
Puff--
SSUUCCKK
KOFF!
HACK!
WHEEZE!

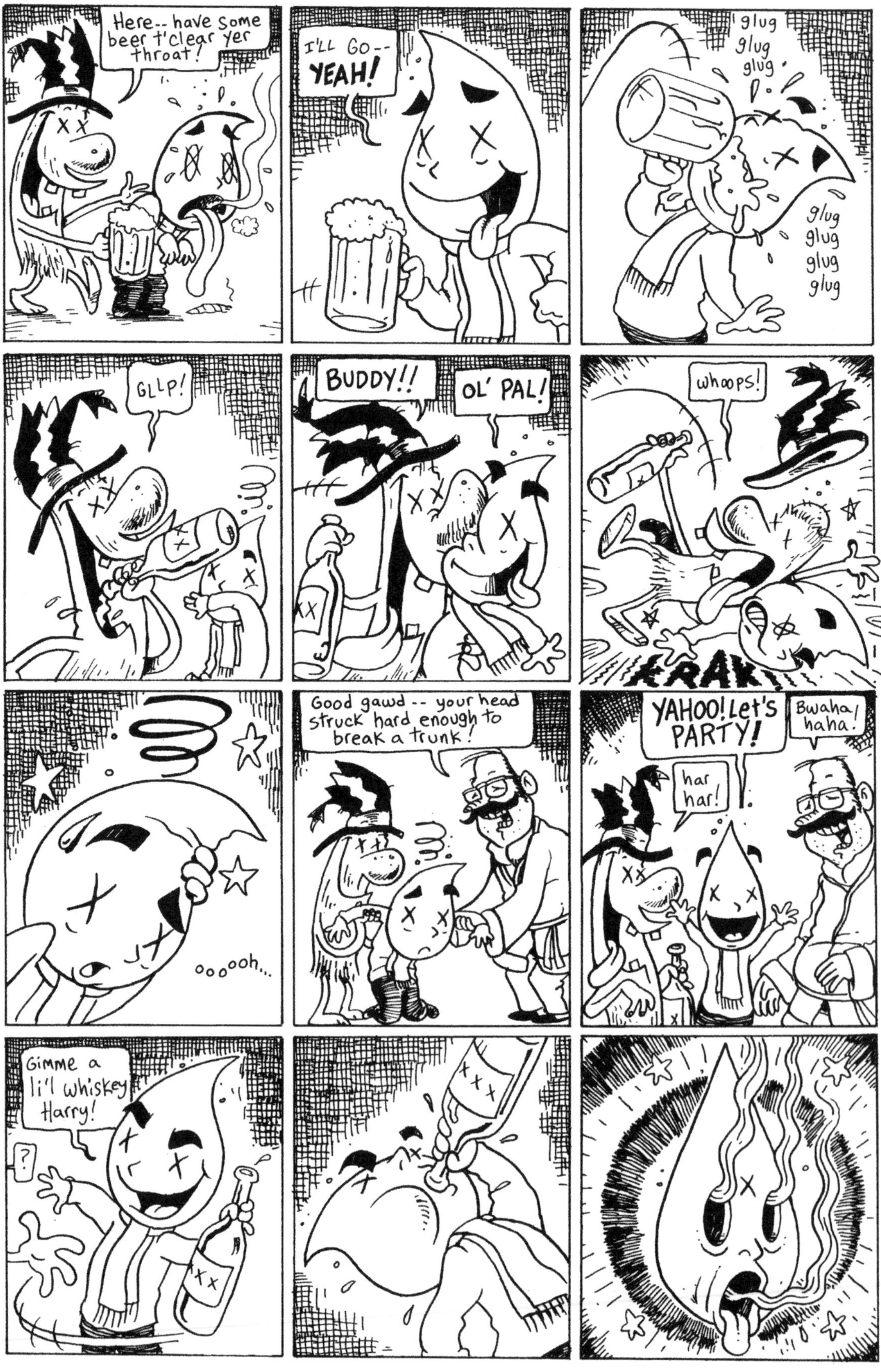
Here-- have some beer t'clear yer throat!
I'LL GO-- YEAH!
glug glug glug
glug glug glug glug
GLLP!
BUDDY!!
OL' PAL!
whoops!
KRAK!
ooooh...
Good gawd -- your head struck hard enough to break a trunk!
YAHOO! Let's PARTY!
har har!
Bwaha haha!
Gimme a li'l whiskey Harry!
?

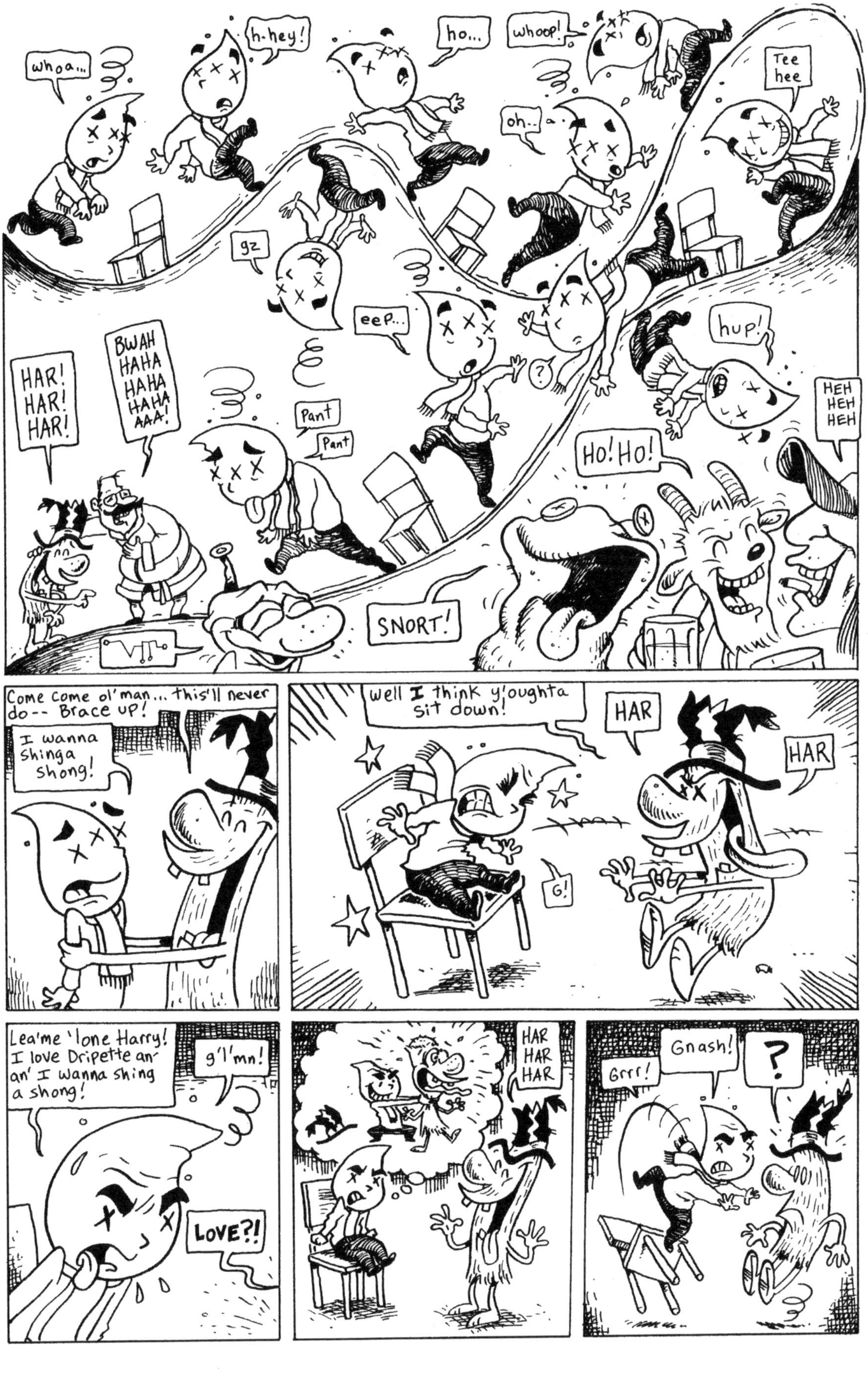
whoa...
h-hey!
ho...
whoop!
Tee hee
oh..
gz
eep...
hup!
HAR! HAR! HAR!
BWAH HAHA HAHA HAHA AAA!
Pant
Pant
Ho! Ho!
HEH HEH HEH
SNORT!
Come come ol' man... this'll never do-- Brace up!
I wanna shinga shong!
well I think y'oughta sit down!
HAR
HAR
G!
Lea'me 'lone Harry! I love Dripette an' an' I wanna shing a shong!
g'l'mn!
LOVE?!
HAR HAR HAR
Grrr!
Gnash!
?

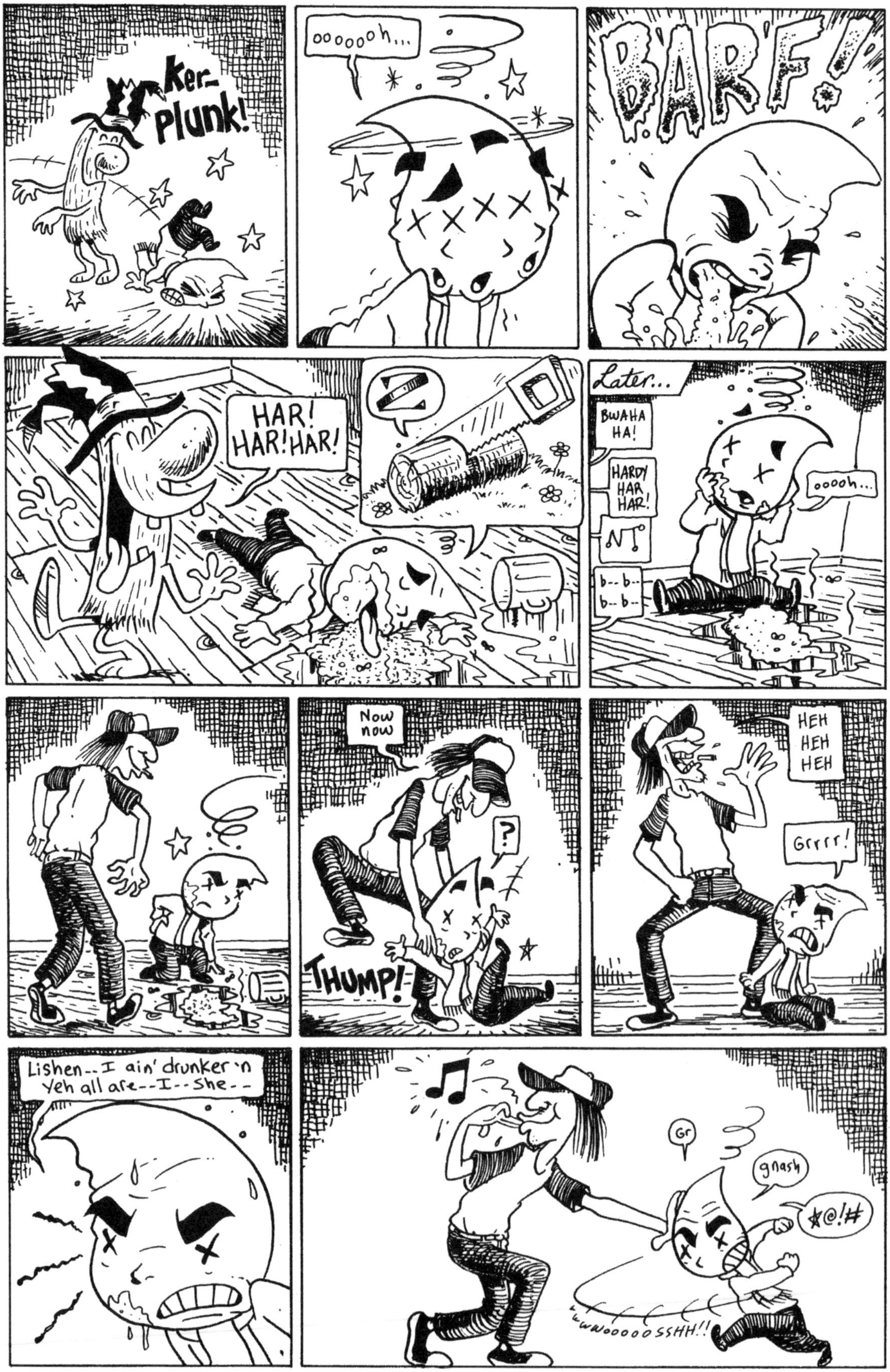
Ker-
Plunk!
oooooooh...
BARF!
HAR! HAR! HAR!
Later...
BWAHA HA!
HARDY HAR HAR!
b-- b--
b-- b--
ooooh...
Now now
?
THUMP!
HEH HEH HEH
Grrrr!
Lishen-- I ain' drunker 'n yeh all are-- I-- She--
Gr
gnash
*@!#
WWOOOOOOSSHH!!

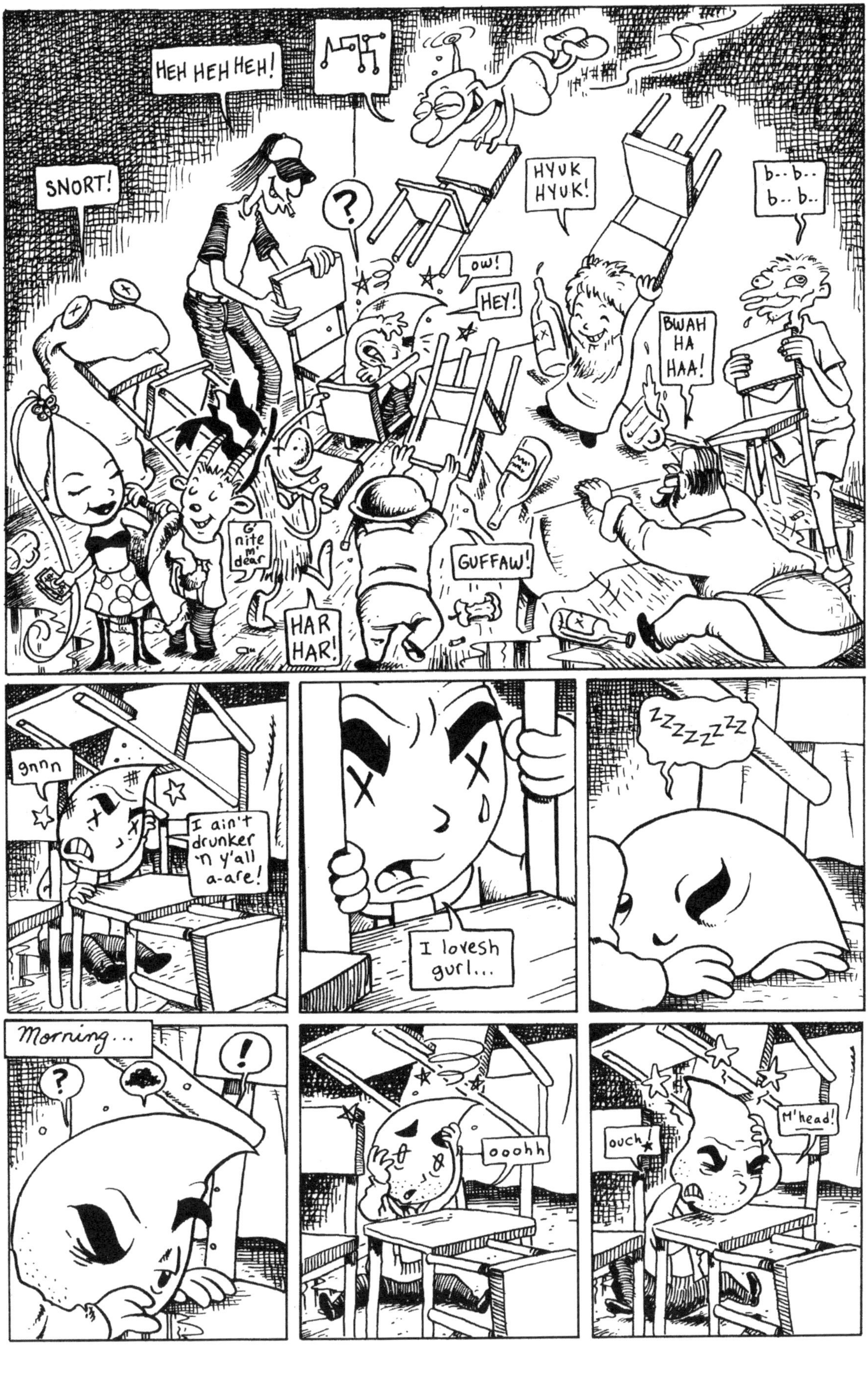
SNORT!
HEH HEH HEH!
?
HYUK HYUK!
b.. b.. b.. b..
OW!
HEY!
BWAH HA HAA!
G' nite m' dear
HAR HAR!
GUFFAW!
gnnn
I ain't drunker 'n y'all a-are!
I lovesh gurl...
ZZZZZZZZ
Morning...
?
!
ooohh
ouch!
M'head!

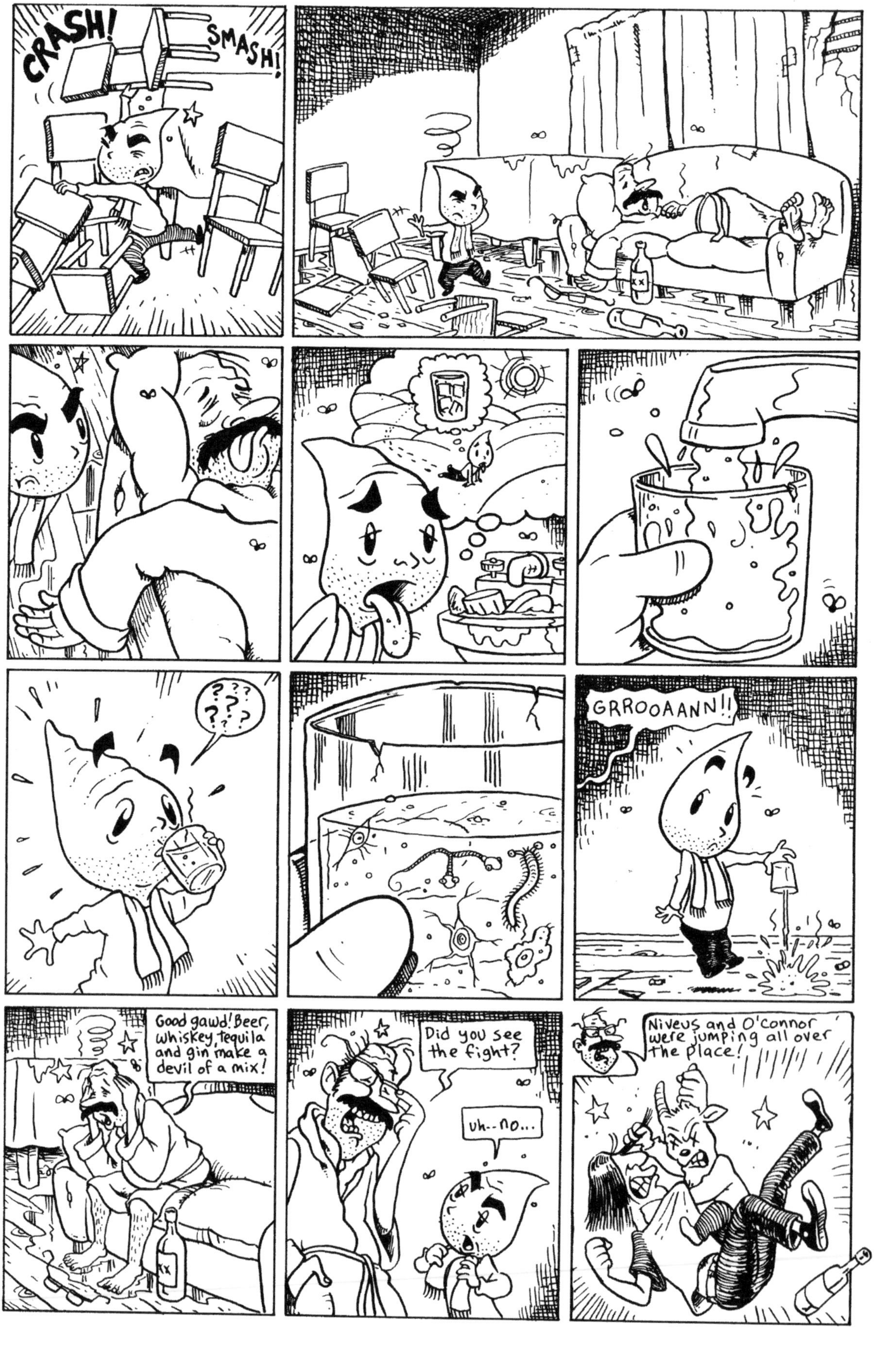
CRASH!
SMASH!
GRROOAANN!!
Good gawd! Beer, whiskey, tequila and gin make a devil of a mix!
Did you see the fight?
uh.. no...
Niveus and O'connor were jumping all over the place!

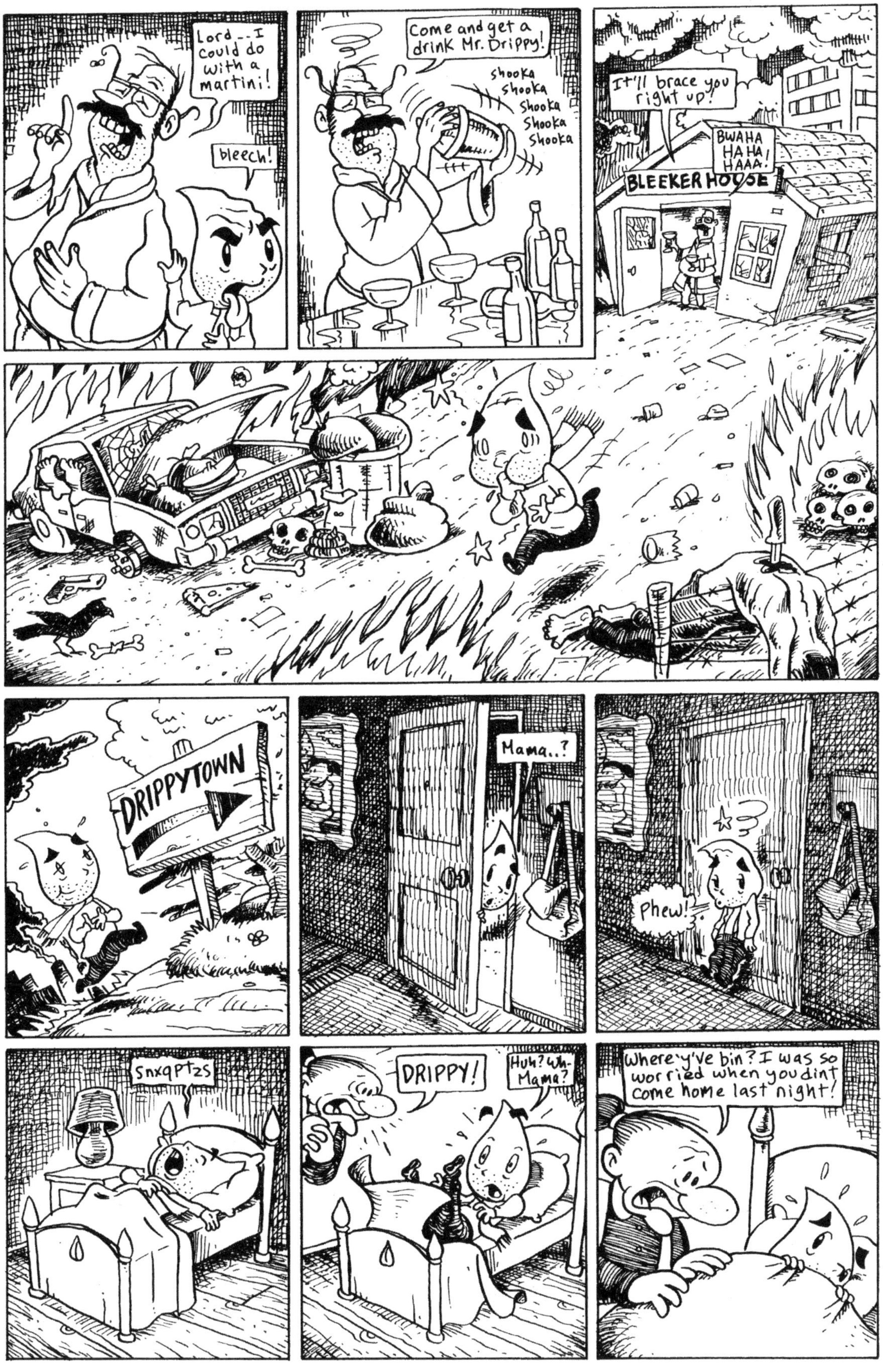

Lord -- I could do with a martini!
bleech!
Come and get a drink Mr. Drippy!
shooka shooka shooka shooka shooka
It'll brace you right up!
BLEEKER HOUSE
BWAHA HA HA! HAAA!
DRIPPYTOWN
Mama..?
Phew!
Snxqptzs
DRIPPY!
Huh? Wh- Mama?
Where y've bin? I was so worried when you dint come home last night!

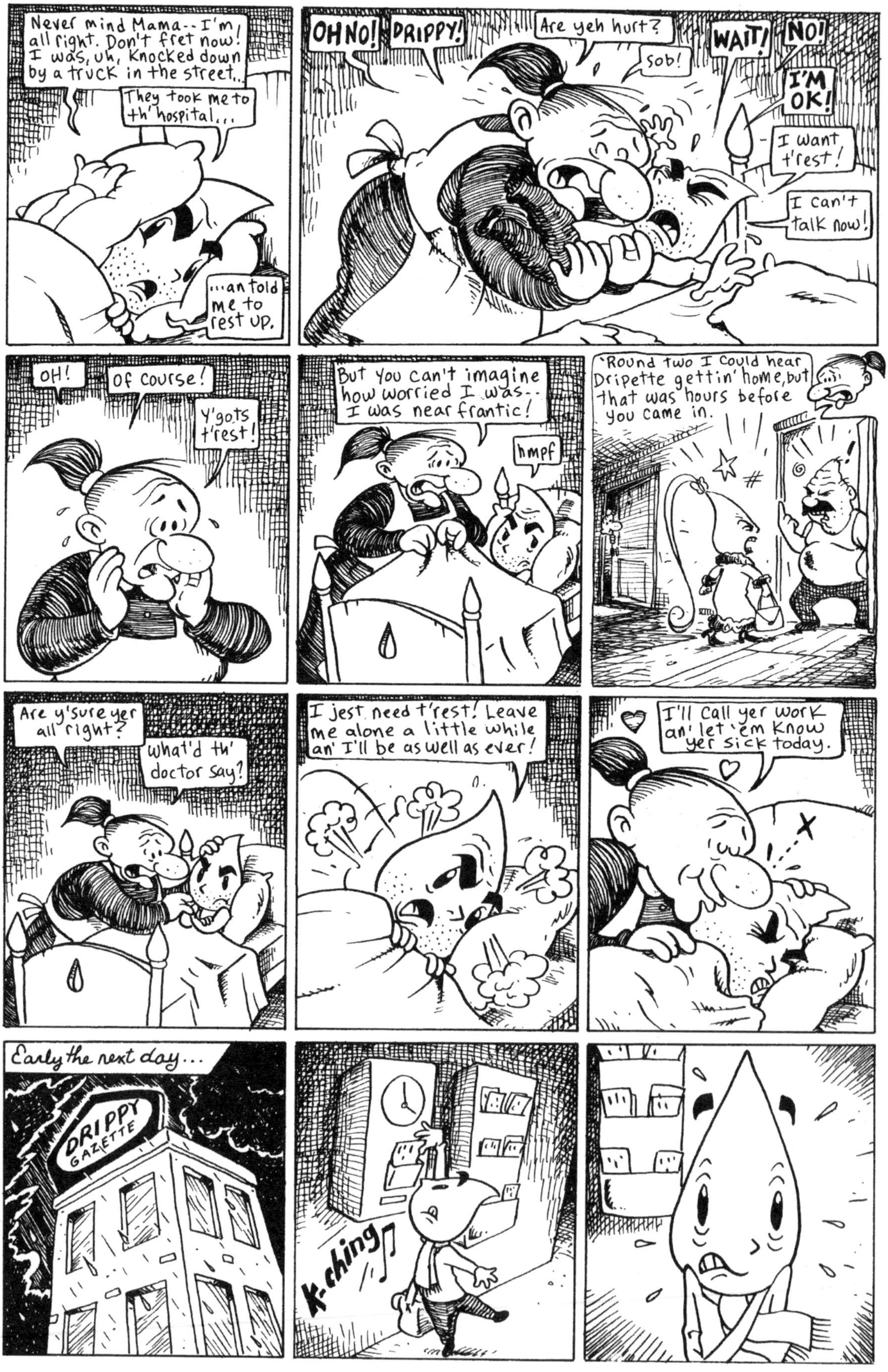
Never mind Mama-- I'm all right. Don't fret now! I was, uh, Knocked down by a truck in the street..
They took me to th' hospital...
...an told me to rest up.
OH NO!
DRIPPY!
Are yeh hurt?
Sob!
WAIT!
NO!
I'M OK!
I want t'rest!
I can't talk now!
OH!
Of course!
Y'gots t'rest!
But you can't imagine how worried I was-- I was near frantic!
hmpf
'Round two I could hear Dripette gettin' home, but that was hours before you came in.
Are y'sure yer all right?
What'd th' doctor say?
I jest need t'rest! Leave me alone a little while an' I'll be as well as ever!
I'll call yer work an' let 'em know yer sick today.
Early the next day...
DRIPPY GAZETTE
K-ching

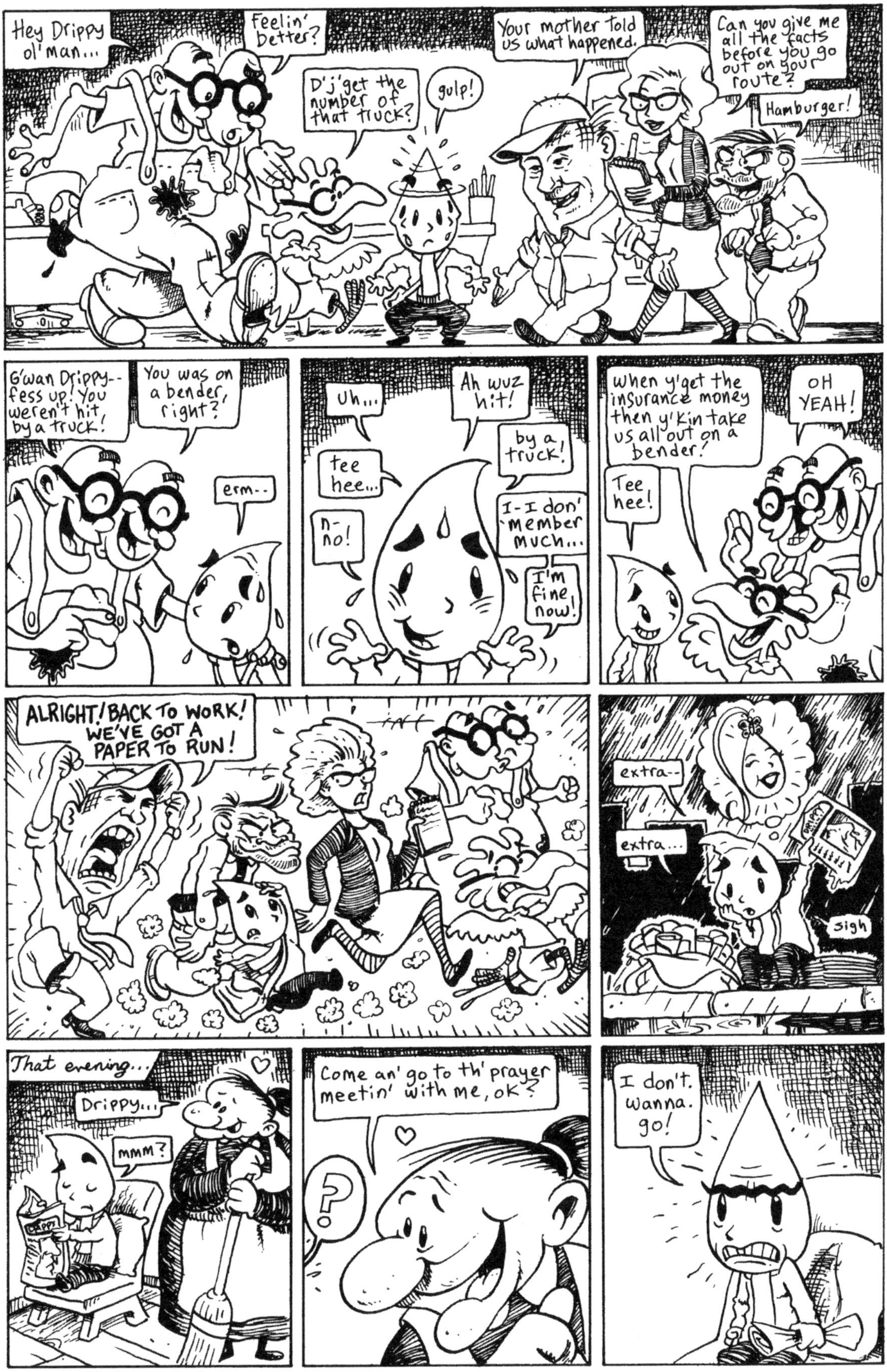

Hey Drippy ol' man...
Feelin' better?
D'j'get the number of that truck?
gulp!
Your mother told us what happened.
Can you give me all the facts before you go out on your route?
Hamburger!
G'wan Drippy-- fess up! You weren't hit by a truck!
You was on a bender, right?
erm--
Uh...
Ah wuz hit!
by a truck!
tee hee...
n-no!
I-I don' member much...
I'm fine now!
When y'get the insurance money then y'kin take us all out on a bender!
OH YEAH!
Tee hee!
ALRIGHT! BACK TO WORK! WE'VE GOT A PAPER TO RUN!
extra--
extra...
sigh
That evening...
Drippy...
mmm?
Come an' go to th' prayer meetin' with me, ok?
?
I don't. wanna. go!

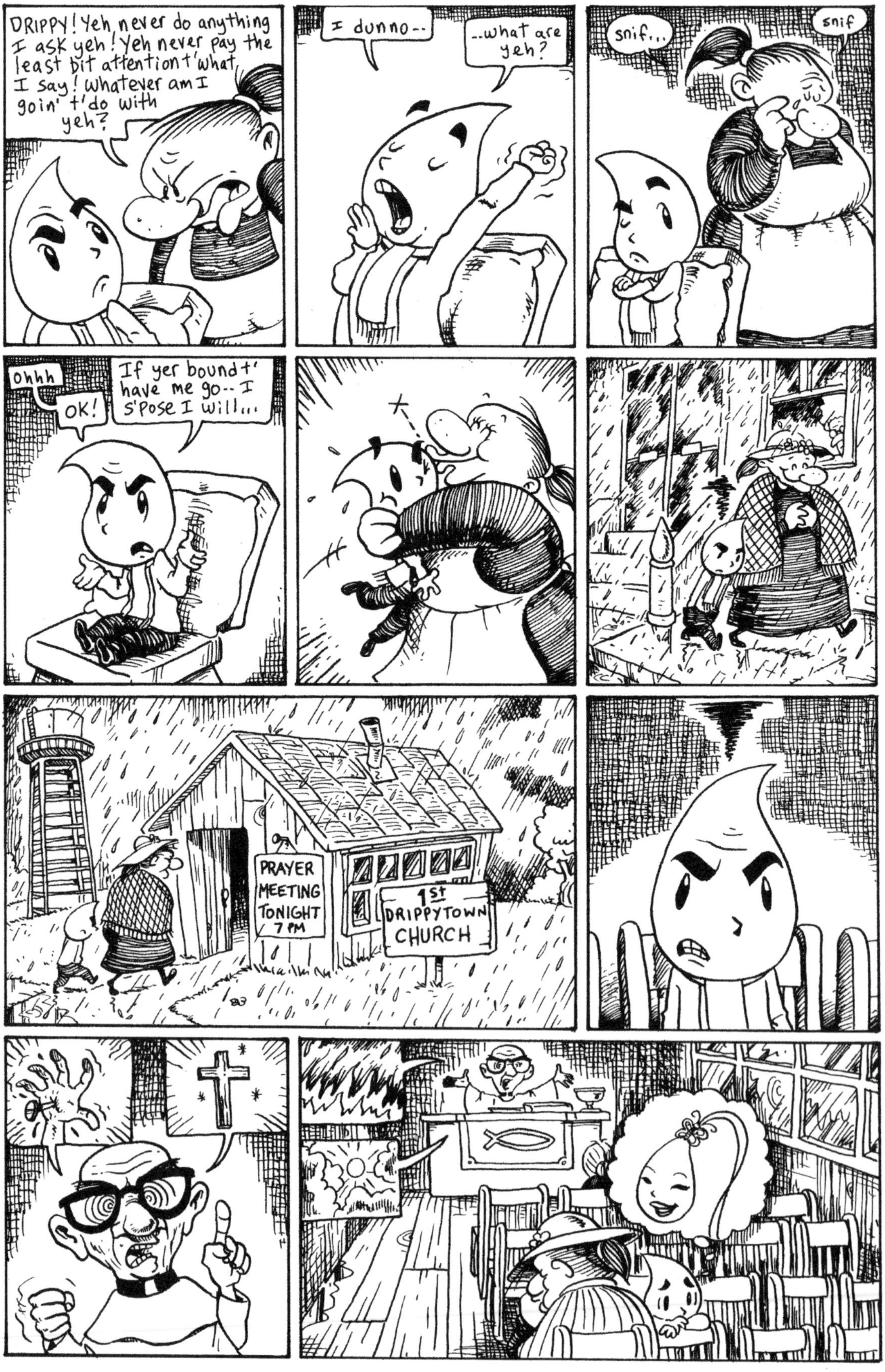

DRIPPY! Yeh never do anything I ask yeh! Yeh never pay the least bit attention t'what I say! Whatever am I goin' t'do with yeh?
I dunno--
..what are yeh?
snif...
snif
Ohhh
OK!
If yer bound t' have me go-- I s'pose I will...
PRAYER MEETING TONIGHT 7 PM
1st DRIPPYTOWN CHURCH

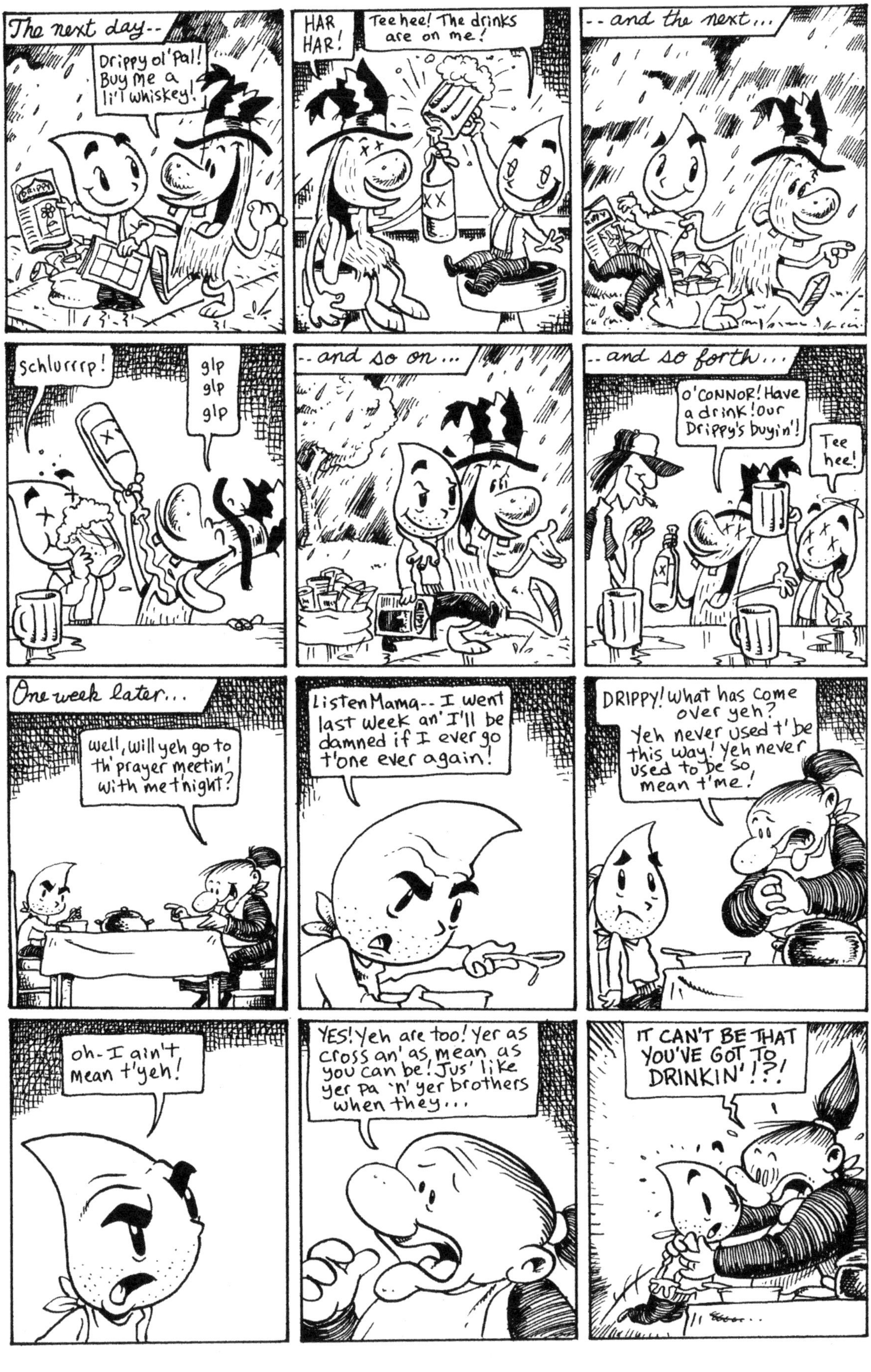
The next day--
Drippy ol' Pal! Buy me a li'l whiskey!
HAR HAR!
Tee hee! The drinks are on me!
--and the next...
Schlurrrp!
glp glp glp
--and so on...
--and so forth...
O'CONNOR! Have a drink! our Drippy's buyin'!
Tee hee!
One week later...
well, will yeh go to th' prayer meetin' with me t'night?
Listen Mama-- I went last week an' I'll be damned if I ever go t'one ever again!
DRIPPY! What has come over yeh? Yeh never used t' be this way! Yeh never used to be so mean t'me!
oh- I ain't mean t'yeh!
YES! Yeh are too! Yer as cross an' as mean as you can be! Jus' like yer Pa 'n' yer brothers when they...
IT CAN'T BE THAT YOU'VE GOT TO DRINKIN'!?!

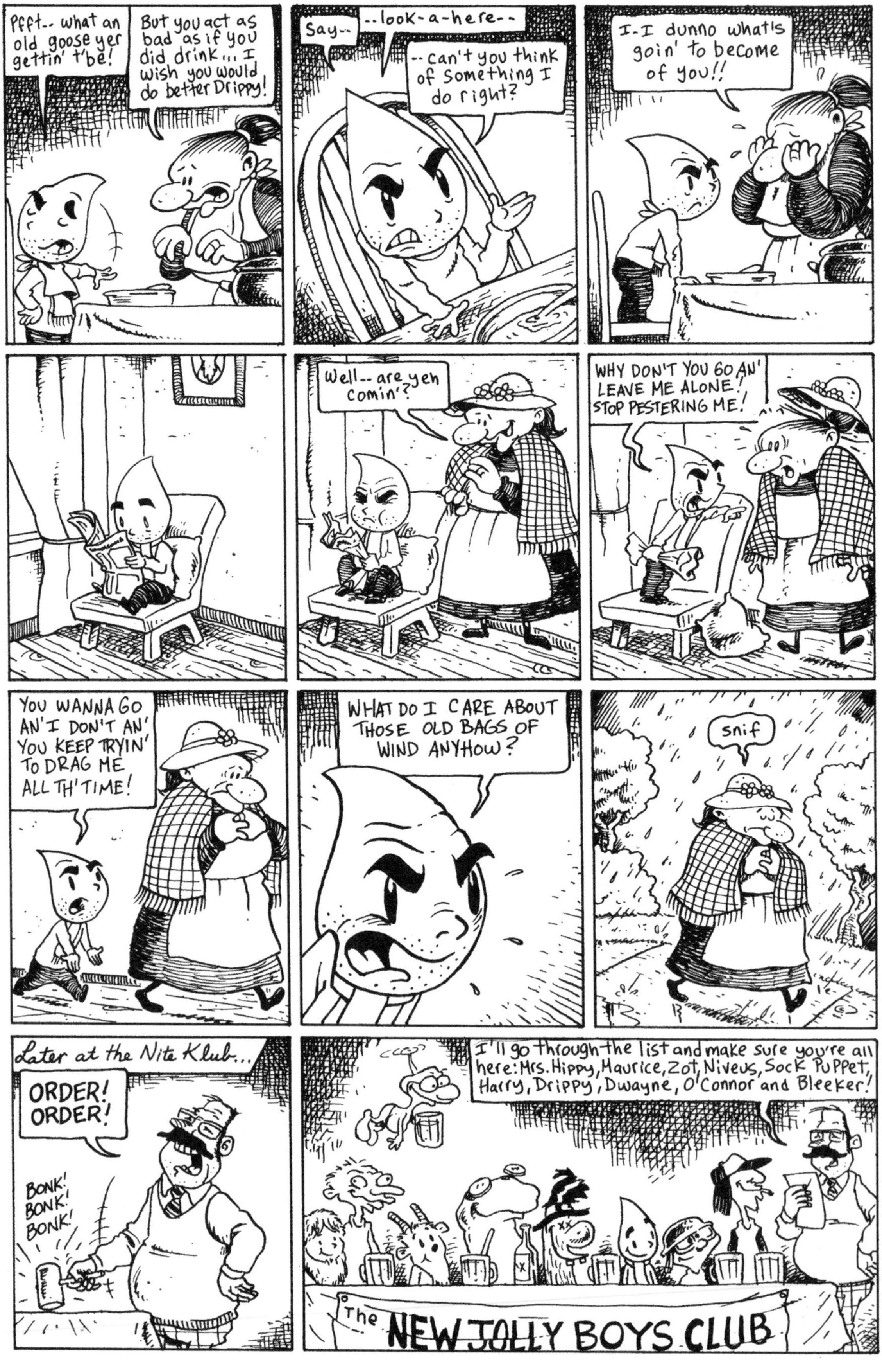
Pfft-- what an old goose yer gettin' t'be!
But you act as bad as if you did drink... I wish you would do better Drippy!
Say--
--look-a-here--
--can't you think of something I do right?
I-I dunno what's goin' to become of you!!
Well-- are yeh comin'?
WHY DON'T YOU GO AN' LEAVE ME ALONE! STOP PESTERING ME!
YOU WANNA GO AN' I DON'T AN' YOU KEEP TRYIN' TO DRAG ME ALL TH' TIME!
WHAT DO I CARE ABOUT THOSE OLD BAGS OF WIND ANYHOW?
snif
Later at the Nite Klub...
ORDER! ORDER!
BONK! BONK! BONK!
I'll go through the list and make sure you're all here: Mrs. Hippy, Maurice, Zot, Niveus, Sock Puppet, Harry, Drippy, Dwayne, O'Connor and Bleeker!
The NEW JOLLY BOYS CLUB

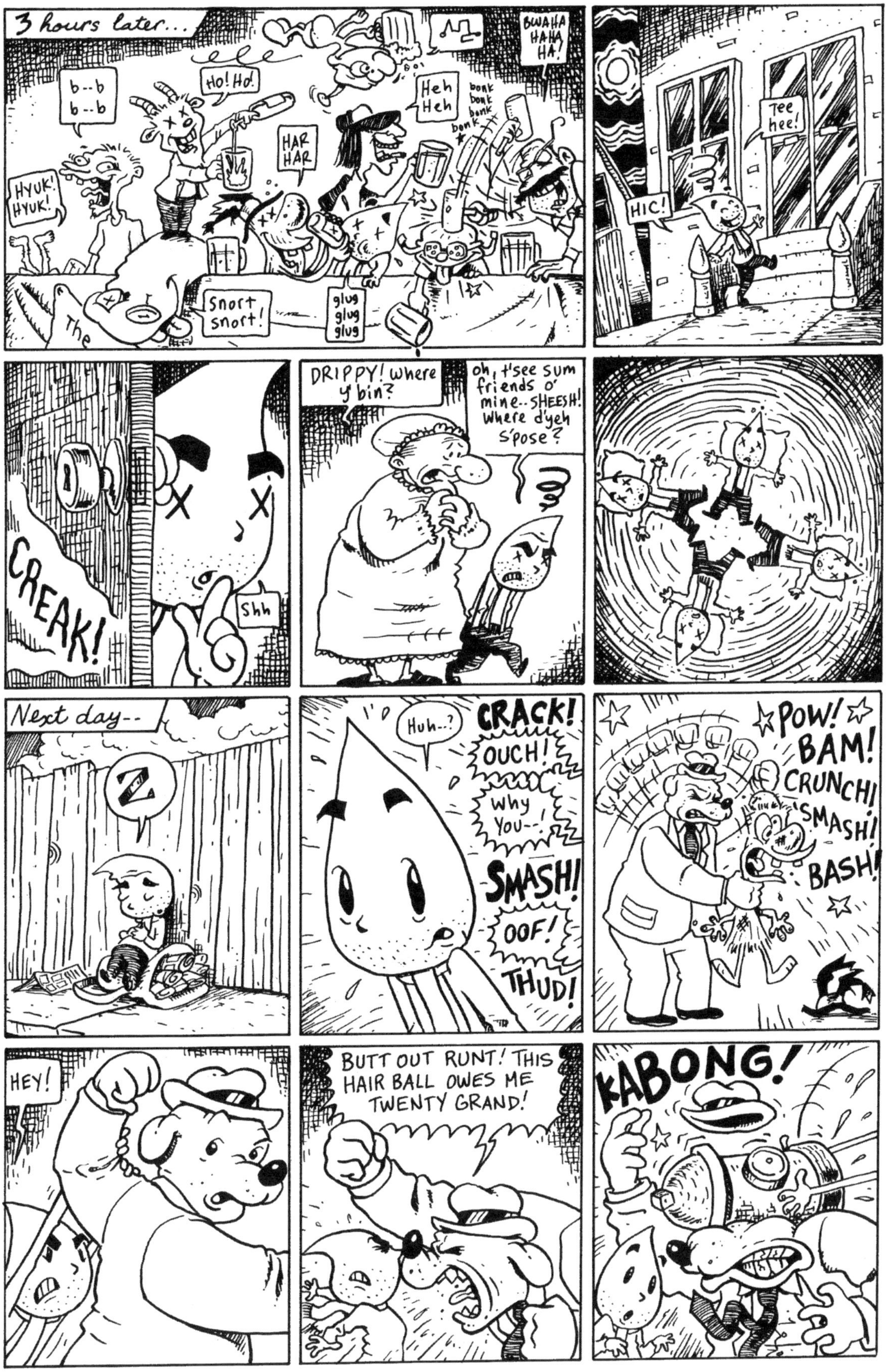
3 hours later...
BWAHA HAHA HA!
b--b b--b
Ho! Ho!
Heh Heh
bonk bonk bonk bonk
HAR HAR
HYUK! HYUK!
Snort snort!
glug glug glug
Tee hee!
HIC!
CREAK!
Shh
DRIPPY! where y' bin?
oh, t'see sum friends o' mine..SHEESH! where d'yeh s'pose?
Next day--
Huh--?
CRACK!
OUCH!
Why You--!
SMASH!
OOF!
THUD!
POW!
BAM!
CRUNCH!
SMASH!
BASH!
HEY!
BUTT OUT RUNT! THIS HAIR BALL OWES ME TWENTY GRAND!
KABONG!

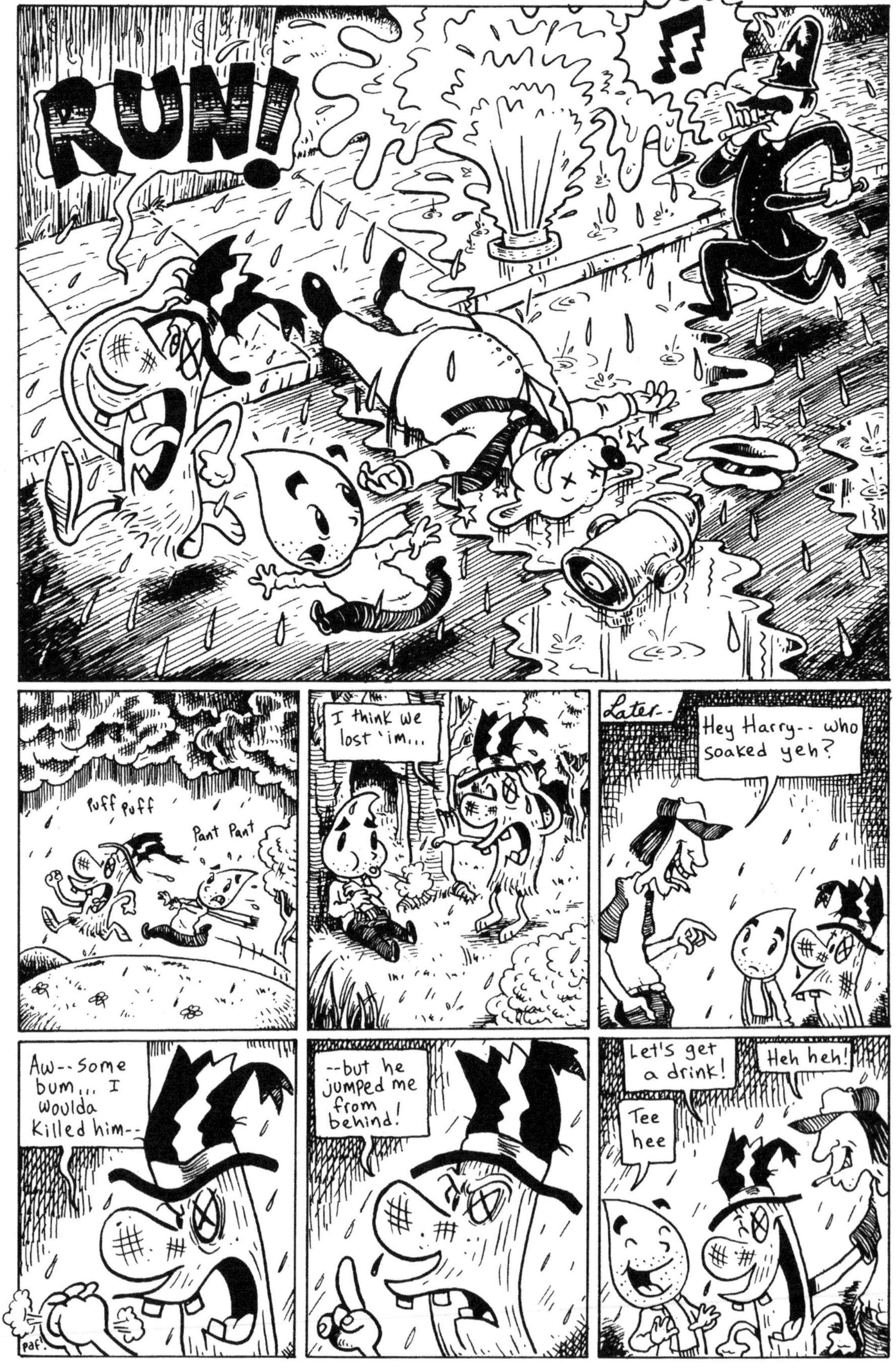
RUN!
Puff puff
Pant Pant
I think we lost 'im...
Later--
Hey Harry-- who soaked yeh?
Aw--some bum... I woulda killed him--
paf!
--but he jumped me from behind!
Let's get a drink!
Heh heh!
Tee hee

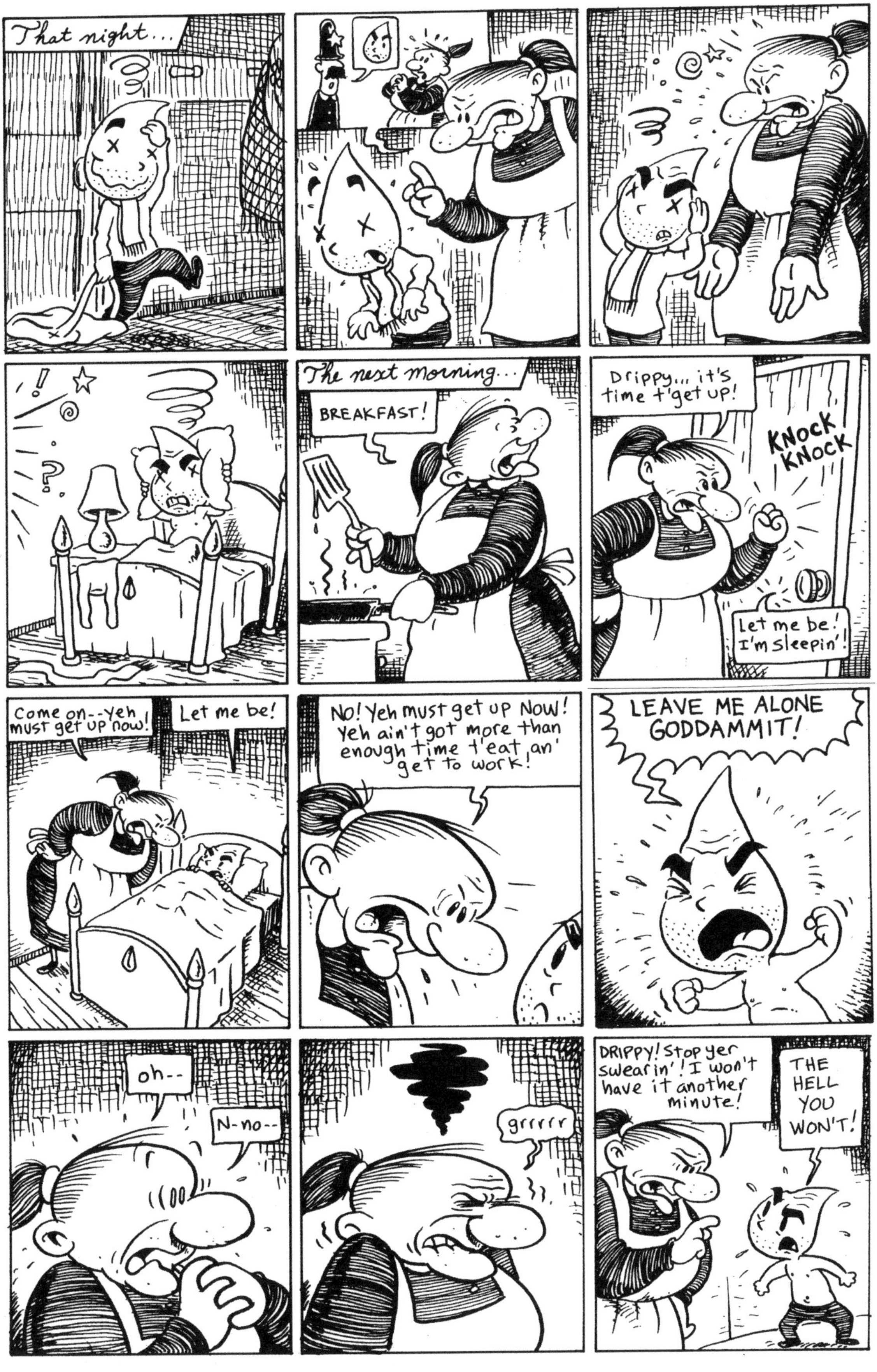
That night...
The next morning...
BREAKFAST!
Drippy... it's time t'get up!
KNOCK KNOCK
Let me be! I'm sleepin'!
Come on--Yeh must get up now!
Let me be!
No! Yeh must get up NOW! Yeh ain't got more than enough time t'eat an' get to work!
LEAVE ME ALONE GODDAMMIT!
oh--
N-no--
grrrrr
DRIPPY! Stop yer swearin'! I won't have it another minute!
THE HELL YOU WON'T!

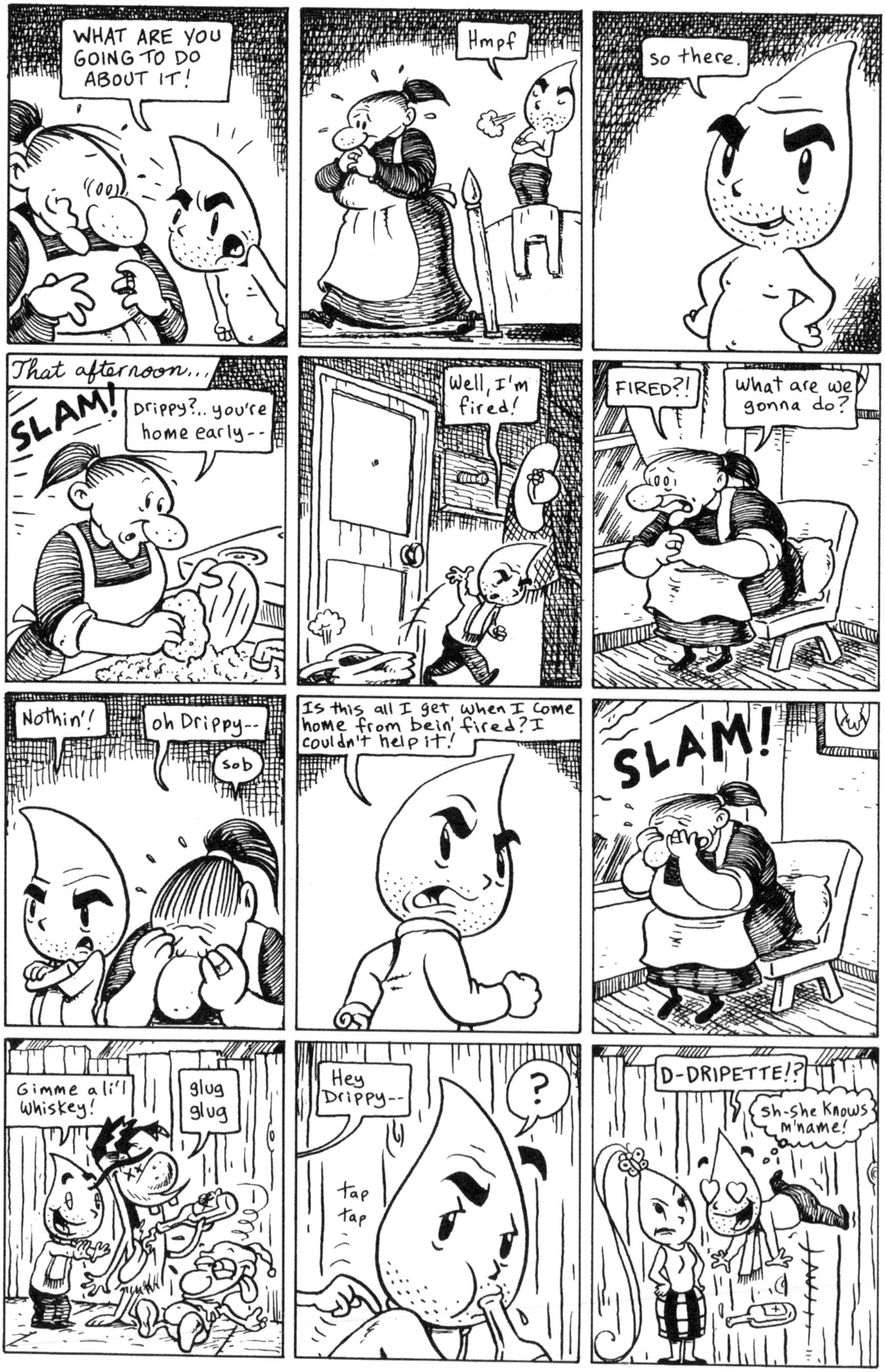
WHAT ARE YOU GOING TO DO ABOUT IT!
Hmpf
so there.
That afternoon...
SLAM!
Drippy?.. you're home early--
Well, I'm fired!
FIRED?!
What are we gonna do?
Nothin'!
oh Drippy--
sob
Is this all I get when I come home from bein' fired? I couldn't help it!
SLAM!
Gimme a li'l whiskey!
glug glug
Hey Drippy--
?
tap tap
D-DRIPETTE!?
sh-she knows m'name!

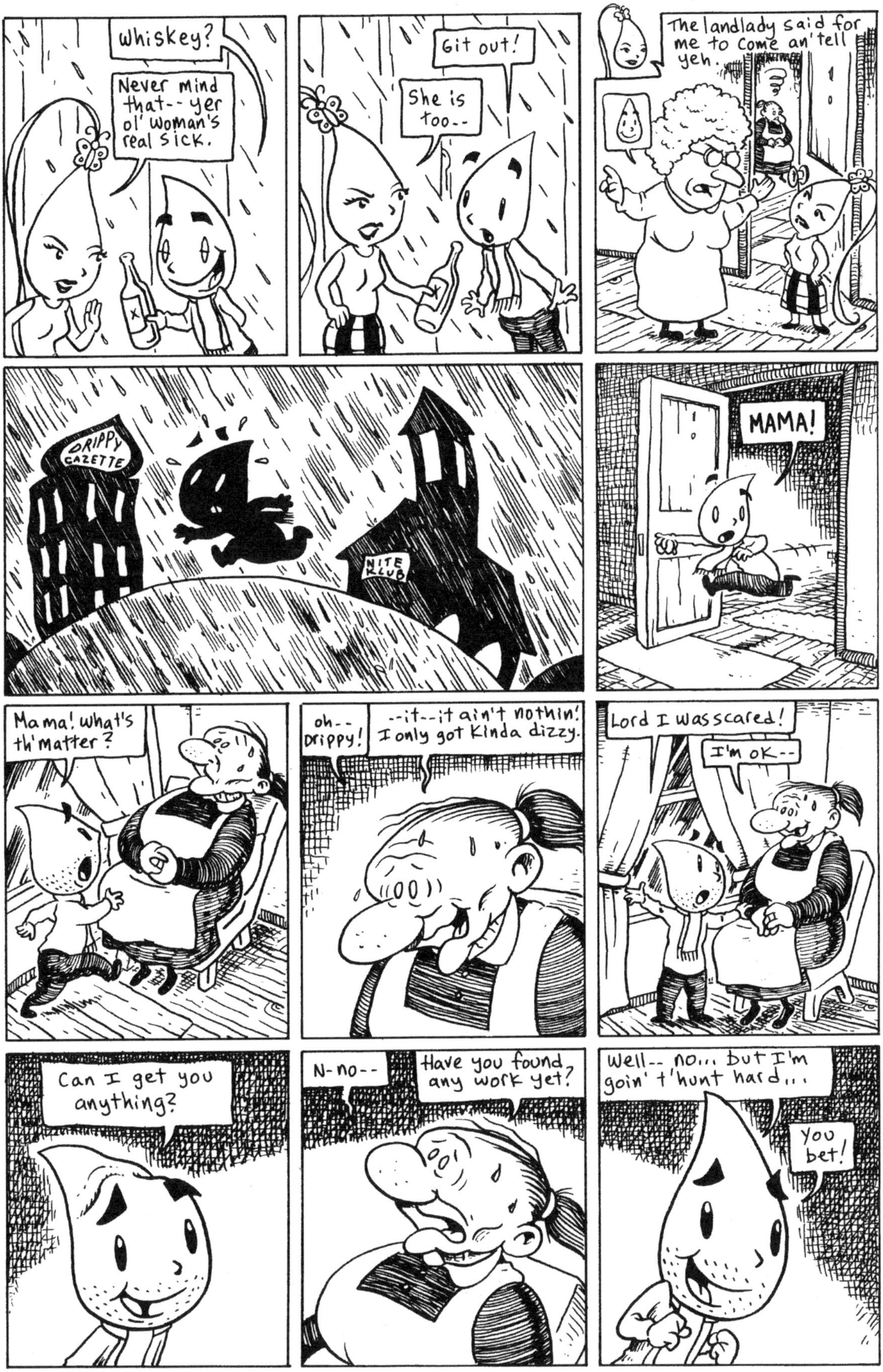
Whiskey?
Never mind that-- yer ol' woman's real sick.
Git out!
She is too--
The landlady said for me to come an' tell yeh.
DRIPPY GAZETTE
NITE KLUB
MAMA!
Mama! what's th' matter?
oh-- Drippy!
--it--it ain't nothin! I only got kinda dizzy.
Lord I was scared!
I'm OK--
Can I get you anything?
N-no--
Have you found any work yet?
Well-- no... But I'm goin' t'hunt hard...
You bet!

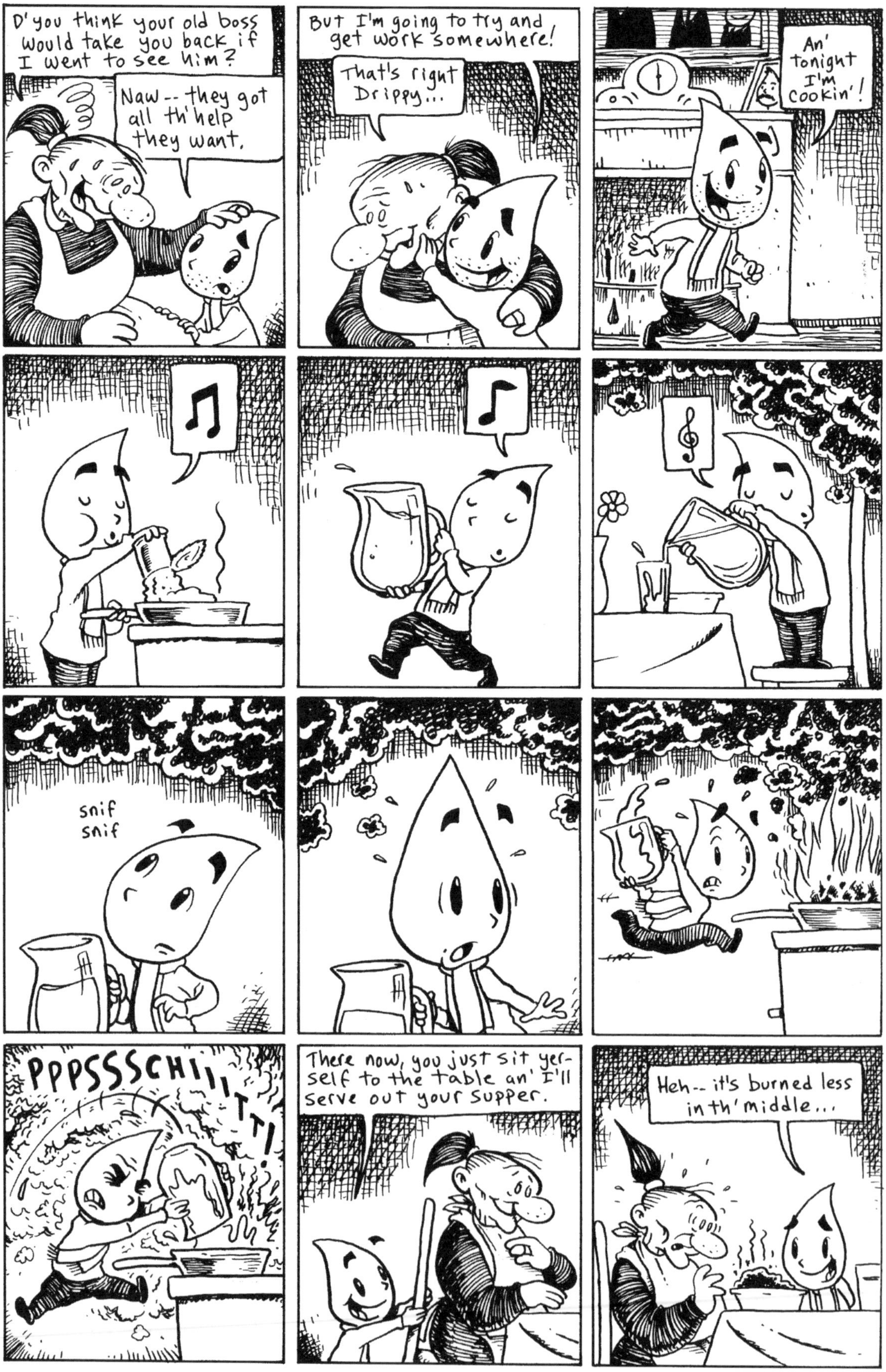
D'you think your old boss would take you back if I went to see him?
Naw -- they got all th' help they want.
But I'm going to try and get work somewhere!
That's right Drippy...
An' tonight I'm cookin'!
snif snif
PPPSSSCHIIITTT!
There now, you just sit yer-self to the table an' I'll serve out your supper.
Heh -- it's burned less in th' middle...

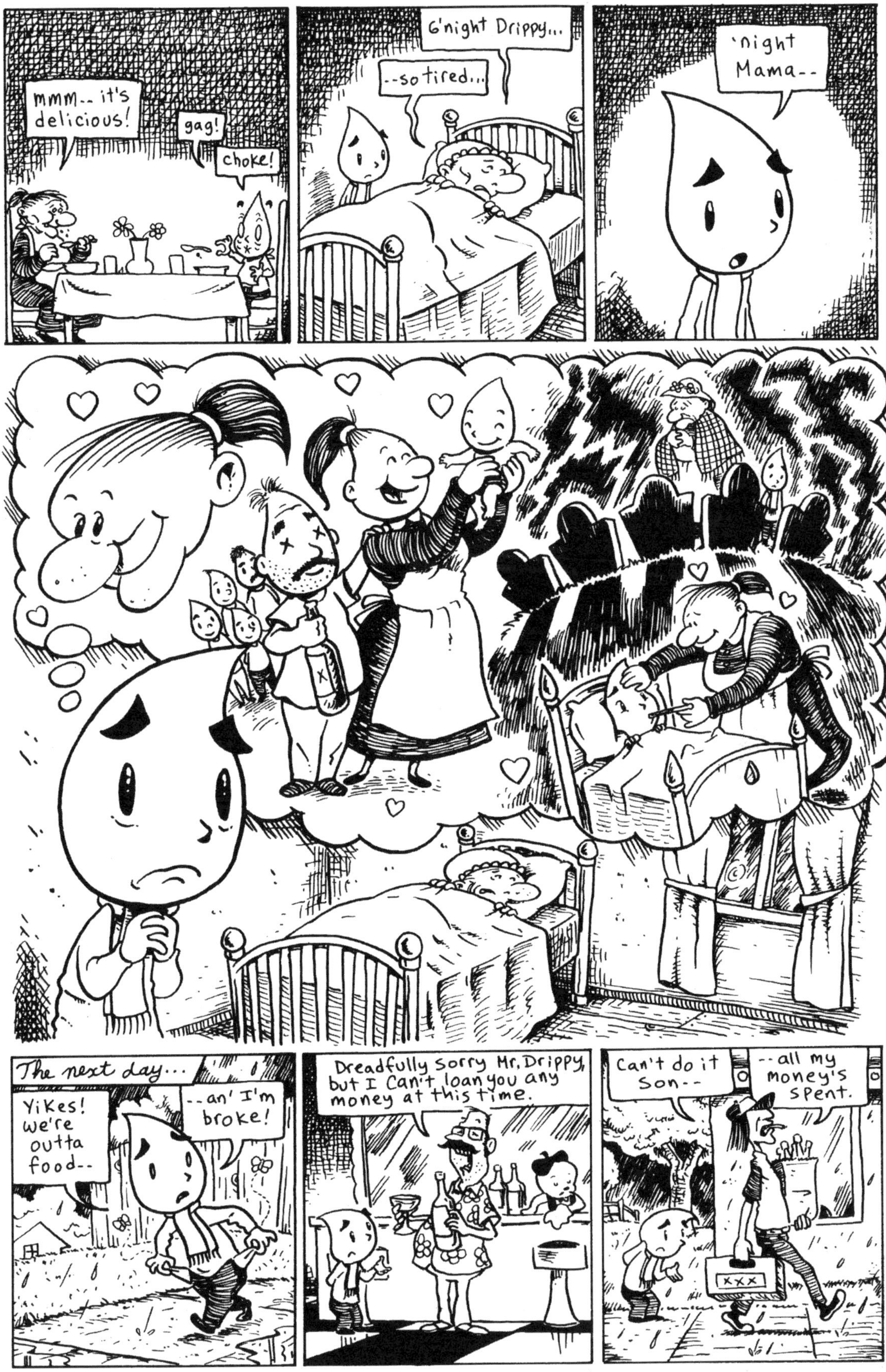
mmm.. it's delicious!
gag!
choke!
G'night Drippy...
--so tired...
'night Mama--
The next day...
Yikes! we're outta food--
--an' I'm broke!
Dreadfully sorry Mr. Drippy, but I can't loan you any money at this time.
Can't do it Son--
--all my money's spent.

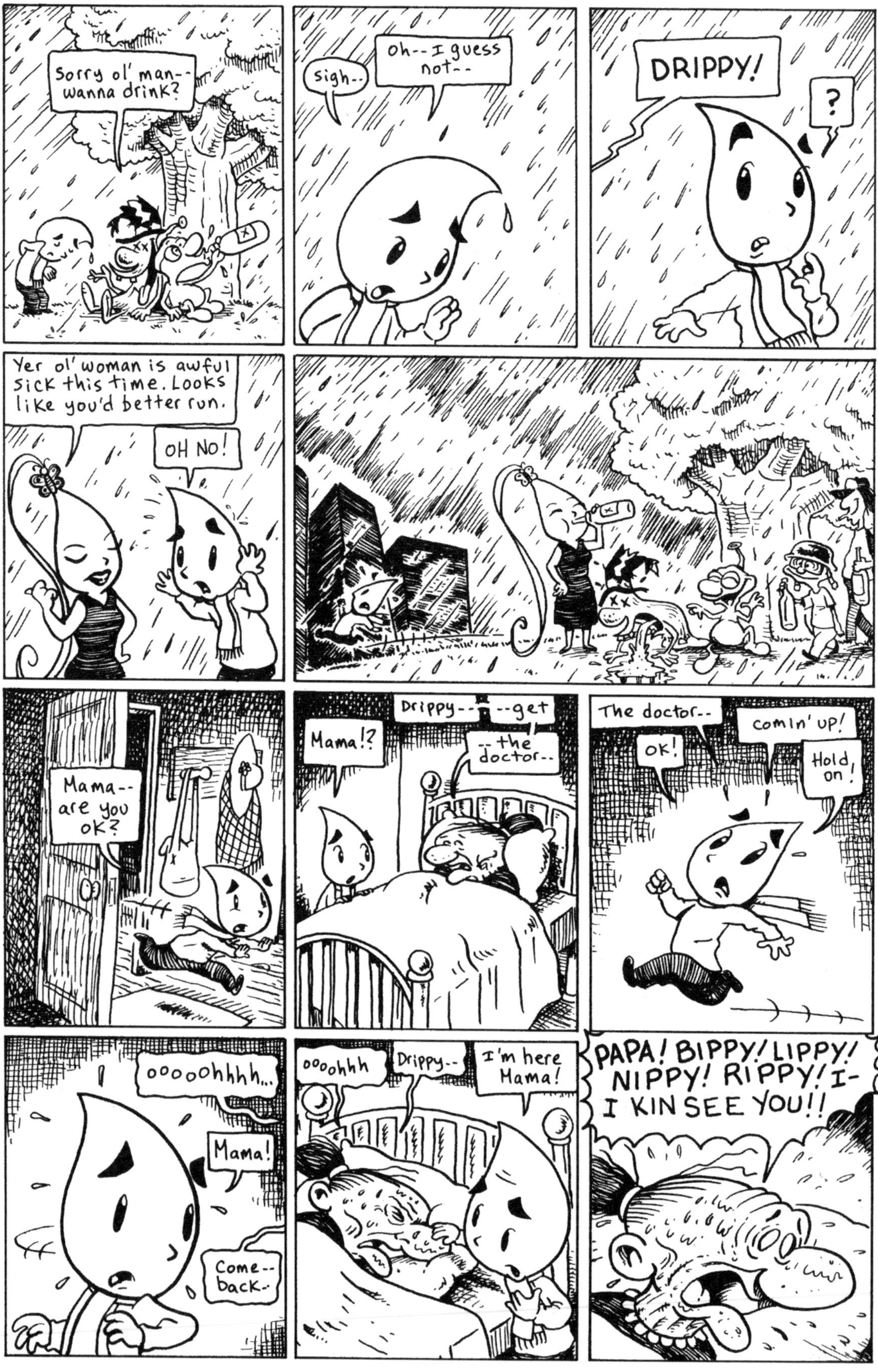
Sorry ol' man--
wanna drink?
sigh--
Oh--I guess not--
DRIPPY!
?
Yer ol' woman is awful sick this time. Looks like you'd better run.
OH NO!
Mama--
are you
OK?
Mama!?
Drippy--
--get
--the
doctor--
The doctor--
OK!
comin' up!
Hold on!
oooooh hhh...
Mama!
Come--
back--
oooohhh
Drippy--
I'm here
Mama!
PAPA! BIPPY! LIPPY!
NIPPY! RIPPY! I-
I KIN SEE YOU!!

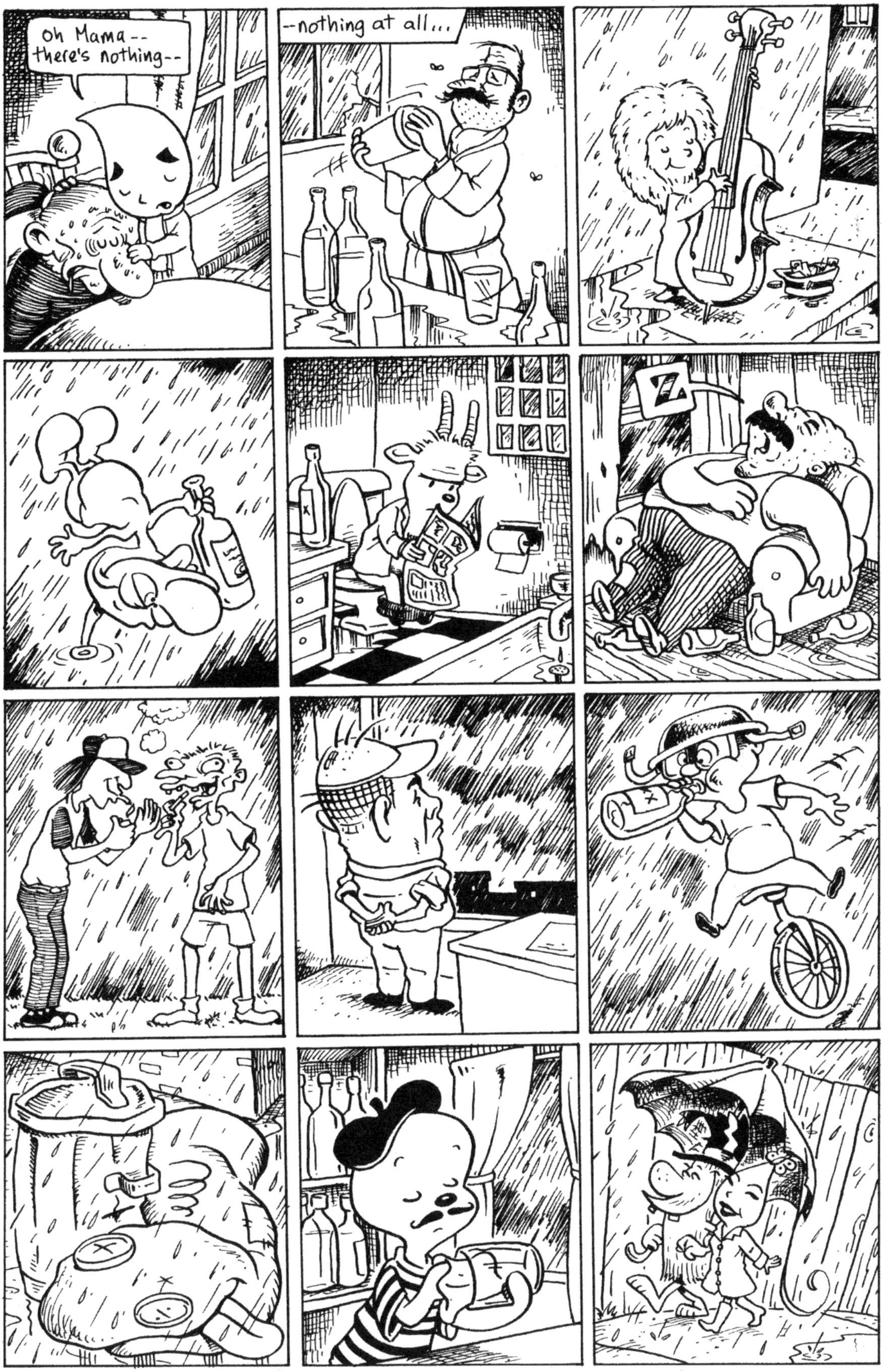
oh Mama-- there's nothing--
--nothing at all...
Z

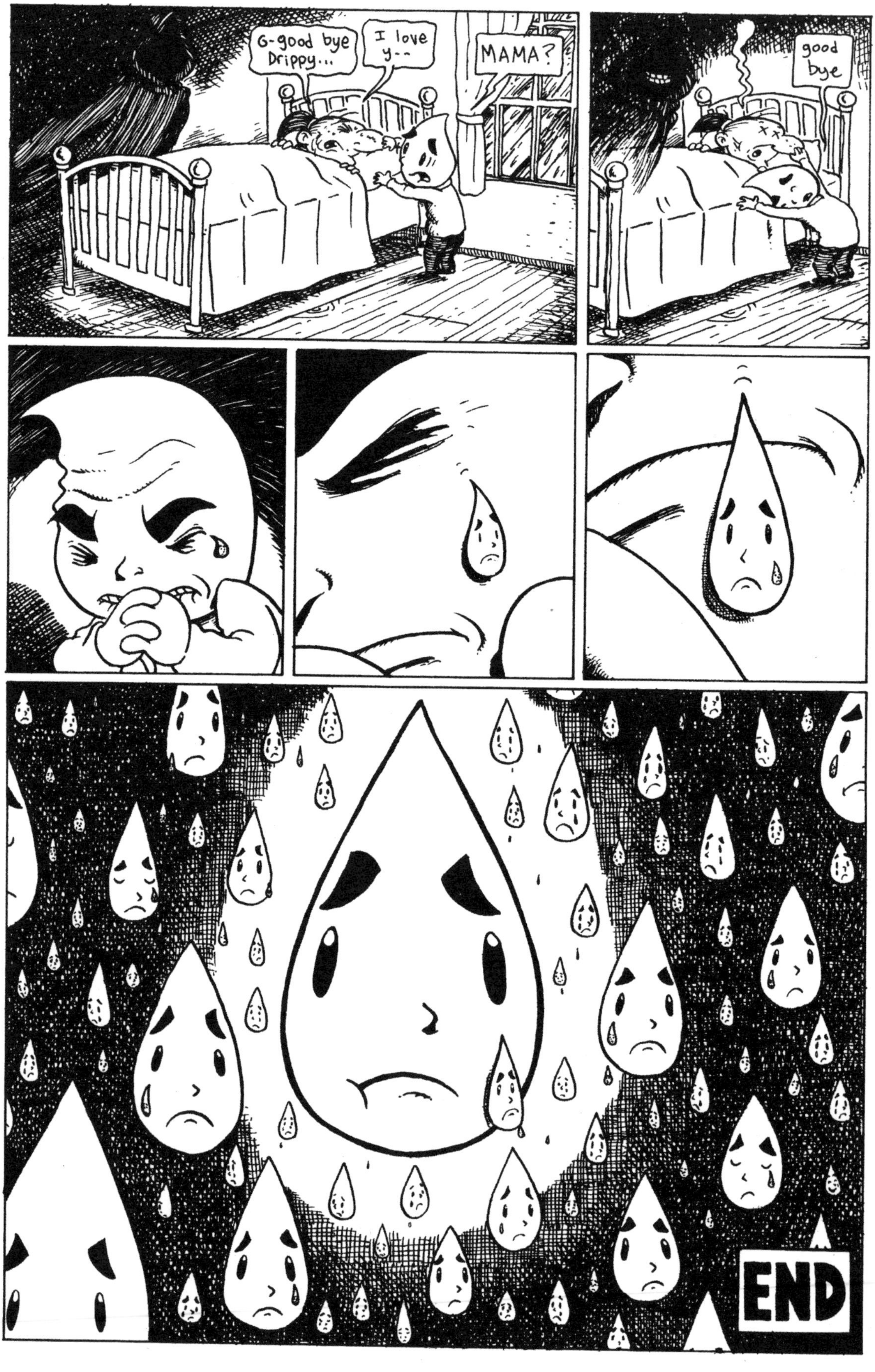
G-good bye Drippy...
I love y--
MAMA?
good bye
END

First Edition
Printed by Gauvin, Gatineau, Quebec, Canada

FSC
www.fsc.org
MIX
Paper from responsible sources
FSC® C100212

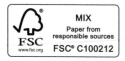

Julian Lawrence was born in
England, grew up in Québec and now
lives in Vancouver, Colombie-Britannique.
www.julianlawrence.net